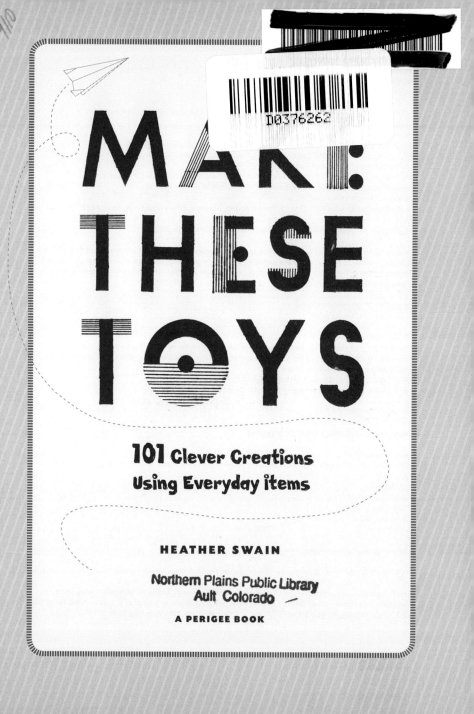

MAKE THESE TOYS

101 Clever Creations
Using Everyday items

HEATHER SWAIN

Northern Plains Public Library
Ault Colorado

A PERIGEE BOOK

A PERIGEE BOOK
Published by the Penguin Group
Penguin Group (USA) Inc.
375 Hudson Street, New York, New York 10014, USA
Penguin Group (Canada), 90 Eglinton Avenue East, Suite 700, Toronto, Ontario M4P 2Y3, Canada
(a division of Pearson Penguin Canada Inc.)
Penguin Books Ltd., 80 Strand, London WC2R 0RL, England
Penguin Group Ireland, 25 St. Stephen's Green, Dublin 2, Ireland (a division of Penguin Books Ltd.)
Penguin Group (Australia), 250 Camberwell Road, Camberwell, Victoria 3124, Australia
(a division of Pearson Australia Group Pty. Ltd.)
Penguin Books India Pvt. Ltd., 11 Community Centre, Panchsheel Park, New Delhi—110 017, India
Penguin Group (NZ), 67 Apollo Drive, Rosedale, North Shore 0632, New Zealand
(a division of Pearson New Zealand Ltd.)
Penguin Books (South Africa) (Pty.) Ltd., 24 Sturdee Avenue, Rosebank, Johannesburg 2196, South Africa

Penguin Books Ltd., Registered Offices: 80 Strand, London WC2R 0RL, England

While the author has made every effort to provide accurate telephone numbers and Internet addresses at the time of
publication, neither the publisher nor the author assumes any responsibility for errors, or for changes that occur after
publication. Further, the publisher does not have any control over and does not assume any responsibility for author
or third-party websites or their content.

Copyright © 2010 by Heather Swain
Text design by Pauline Neuwirth

All rights reserved.
No part of this book may be reproduced, scanned, or distributed in any printed or electronic form without
permission. Please do not participate in or encourage piracy of copyrighted materials in violation of the author's
rights. Purchase only authorized editions.
PERIGEE is a registered trademark of Penguin Group (USA) Inc.
The "P" design is a trademark belonging to Penguin Group (USA) Inc.

First edition: July 2010

Library of Congress Cataloging-in-Publication Data

Swain, Heather, 1969–
    Make these toys : 101 clever creations using everyday items / Heather Swain.
        p.   cm.
    Includes index.
    ISBN 978-0-399-53591-8
    1. Toy making. I. Title.
    TT174.S86   2010
    745.592'4—dc22   2010002461

PRINTED IN THE UNITED STATES OF AMERICA

10 9 8 7 6 5 4 3 2 1

Most Perigee books are available at special quantity discounts for bulk purchases for sales promotions, premiums,
fund-raising, or educational use. Special books, or book excerpts, can also be created to fit specific needs. For details,
write: Special Markets, Penguin Group (USA) Inc., 375 Hudson Street, New York, New York 10014.

For Clementine and Graham

Acknowledgments

I could no more write this book without the following people in my life than I could make a mini-marshmallow popper without paper cups and balloons:

- Barbara Swain—creative, resourceful mom who taught me the art of playing
- Richard Swain—supportive father who loves to save a buck
- Dan Vonnegut—husband who doesn't mind when I make a mess because he believes (even before I do) that I'll make something interesting
- Clementine and Graham—kids who fill my day with wonder and are the inspiration for everything I make
- Lucinda Brown—former fluids gal whose engineering background was indispensable to the creation of the windup toys
- Stephanie Kip-Rostan—superagent who helped form the idea for this book
- Monika Verma—superagent's right-hand gal who keeps track of all the details
- Meg Leder—editor extraordinaire who made this book possible
- Perigee staff—the people who turned the idea into reality
- Becky, Em, and LJ—my playmates and personal cheerleaders who keep me sane when all my screws have fallen under the table and I can't find the glue stick

Contents

introduction

KIDS TODAY CAN get virtually any plaything their little hearts desire by jumping online (either virtually via the Internet or by going old-school and standing in line at the local toy store). And yet, years ago, before mega toy stores and Internet shopping, kids found plenty of ways to entertain themselves. Children have been playing with rag dolls, slingshots, sewing cards, and wooden hoops with sticks since homesteaders parked their Conestoga wagons on the prairies. Most of these playthings were made by either the kids themselves or the grown-ups who loved them. Even though we don't have to make toys for kids anymore, there are still plenty of good reasons to make toys at home.

1. Making Toys Saves Money

As with most things in life, if you make your fun rather than buy it, you'll save a few bucks. I'm not talking whittling wooden heirlooms from trees you fell on the back forty or building elaborate motorized models from an old radio you took apart (neither of which I'm savvy enough or patient enough to do). My family has a playroom filled with toys, most of which come from stores because either they were gifts or we decided they were worth the money. In this book, I'm talking mostly about replacing that cheap mass-manufactured junk (the kind that circulates through the toy store shelves, into our homes, and straight to the landfill after it breaks twenty-four seconds after use) with stuff you can make yourself because fun doesn't have to come in a box. Sometimes fun *is* a box. And boxes are cheap.

2. Making Toys Conserves Resources

Maybe you don't mind the couple hundred bucks you might save if you made propeller boats out of milk cartons and dolls out of old T-shirts. Then how about that tried-and-true recycling motto: Reduce, Reuse, Recycle? You probably already have everything lying around your house that I use in this book and most of it you were going to chuck anyway. So why not make something out of it first, then toss it after the kids have had some fun? At the end of the day, the more toys you make, the less plastic crapola ends up buried in the ground somewhere.

3. Making Toys Means Fewer Toxins in Your Home

Maybe you figure the trash can full of things you'd throw away wouldn't make that big of a difference to the earth when we're all driving SUVs and stinking up the environment anyway. Fair enough, but how about all the reports of toxins in toys, from lead in the paint to BPA in the plastic to tiny magnets that kids might swallow? It's enough to make me want to give my kids a wooden hoop and corncob doll to play with. So, if the safety of toys concerns you, then making toys out of food cartons and fabric, poster board and drinking straws might alleviate some of your worry.

4. Making Toys Is Fun

And if none of that resonates, then how about this: Half the fun of playing with homemade toys is making them. If you're already a crafty person or you'd like to be more of one or if you want to raise kids to be creative and resourceful, then making toys is a simple, inexpensive, safe, and fun place to start. Understanding how to build the things we play with opens doors for imagination and innovation and ultimately teaches us how to entertain ourselves without always spending money.

For me there's one reason that trumps all those others and that's how my kids respond to homemade toys. I've always been pretty crafty around the house, but once I started working on this book and making most of the things my kids play with, an interesting thing happened. Now, instead of asking me to buy them toys, first they ask me if I can make them something. And sometimes when they're bored, they skip the whining about how they don't have any toys and instead they make something themselves. The first toy my five-year-old daughter made warmed my soul (warning: I will now brag about my child). She drew a picture of me on a wooden craft stick, then drew a picture of herself on a wooden hinged clothespin. She attached the clothespin to the top of the craft stick and said, "See, it's me riding on your shoulders. Now I'm going to make Daddy." I swooned with delight.

So, I like reasons 1, 2, and 3, but to be honest, I consider them merely perks to number 4. And all four reasons point to the biggest one of all: Making toys makes kids happy, which is what playing should be all about.

How to Use This Book

YOU'VE GOT YOUR crafts: flowers pressed in waxed paper, decoupage vases, handprint turkeys, pinecone snowmen.

You've got your toys: plastic-headed dolls that squeal and pee, tiny metal cars with rubber tires, battery-powered bubble blowers, giant plastic playhouses with microwaves and cell phone replicas.

And then you've got your crafty toys.

In my book, a craft is something you make and then it either sits on a shelf for your handiwork to be admired or it has some practical application, like a crocheted poncho. A toy, on the other hand, is something you play with. The process of making it is the first step, one that is usually farmed out to a manufacturer somewhere, unless you get crafty and circumvent the system by making your own toys out of stuff around your house.

This book is set up like a craft book. It's organized by materials—cardboard tubes, balloons, spools, and the like. Each project lists all the materials you will need, followed by step-by-step written instructions and simple line drawings to help you understand the process. When you're done making the project you'll end up with something you and your kids can play with for a while.

Some of the projects are longtime favorites among people who make toys at home, such as kaleidoscopes, clothespin people, and sock babies. Others are reinterpretations of toys you might see in old catalogs or early-twentieth-century toy books, such as the zip-line balloon racer, the stacking box face puzzle, and the shoe box baby carriage. Hopefully, most of what you'll find here will be new takes or fresh ideas for homemade toys, though I'd never claim to be the only one who's ever made these things. If ideas like evolution and electricity were simultaneously discovered by different people, I'm certain someone else in the history of the world has figured out how to make a version of my mini-marshmallow popper.

I've made (and my kids have tested) every project here. I knew quickly which toys were good—the ones my kids couldn't wait to get their grubby paws on—and which ones were duds or would be too delicate to put in the book (see "grubby paws" above). I've done my best to include projects that nearly anyone with opposable thumbs could make, but also some that even advanced crafters with dedicated glue guns and X-Acto knife holsters will relish, plus everything in between. The spectrum of projects include ones kids could make with very little adult supervision up to things adults will want to make with a bit of help from the kids. I've also tried my best to include projects that will appeal to a variety of age groups (or to everyone) and across gender, but I haven't marked any projects with a particular age, gender, or difficulty because I think that depends on who's making and playing with the toys. I did, however, organize projects within each category from the most simple to the most complicated. So look at the beginning of each section for easy ideas and toward the back for a challenge.

You'll find a few extra things in here as well. Each section has facts about the materials being used or the thing you'll be building so if anyone asks you where balloons come from while you're making a zip-line balloon racer, you'll look really smart. On the next few pages, you'll find a complete materials list (think of it like a pantry-stocking shopping list from a cookbook) because you'll use many of these materials several times over. At the end of the book, I've included a glossary of terms for weird things like pony beads and chenille stems, so if you don't know what I'm talking about, check out the back of the book. You'll also find templates so you can trace or copy and cut out the objects used in different projects if drawing isn't your bag. I've also included classic recipes for homemade paints, doughs, bubbles, and the like, which any toy book worth its salt (dough) should have. Finally, I've included an index to help you find the treasures waiting inside.

My hope is that you'll innovate and create your own projects as you go through this book, but mostly I hope you have as much fun as my kids and I have when you make these toys!

Materials List

HERE IS A master list of the materials used in this book. I keep most of this stuff on hand, much as a cook will keep basic ingredients in a well-stocked pantry. You might find that you look differently at your trash and recycling or offerings in the local dollar store after you start making toys—packaging, boxes, bags, food containers, weird little scraps, and odds and ends all make great resources for your own designs.

From Your Art Supplies

chalk (white)
chenille stems
colored pencils
craft sticks
crayons
foam board
glitter
glow-in-the-dark star and planet
  stickers
glue sticks
mirror board
nontoxic markers
paint
paintbrushes
paper (construction and white
  drawing)
pencil (one sharpened for drawing
  and one unsharpened wood type)
permanent markers
poster board
scissors
tape (masking, transparent,
  and duct)
tracing paper
white glue

From Your Craft Supplies

½-inch flat braided elastic (e.g.,
  what you might find inside the
  waistband of a skirt)
elastic cord, round
embroidery floss
embroidery hoop
fabric glue
fabric markers
fabric scraps
felt
flexible measuring tape
googly eyes

grosgrain ribbon or other wide
flat fabric ribbon
heavy-duty craft glue (such as
Gorilla Glue)
iron-on decals
jingle bells
knitting needle
pinking shears
polyfill
pom-poms
pony beads
safety pins
self-adhesive hook-and-loop
fastener tape and dots (aka
Velcro)
sewing needle
sparkly things like sequins,
buttons, and beads
spools
straight pins
thread
yarn

From Your Office Supplies
binder clips
circular reinforcement labels
hole punch
manila file folders
paper clips
prong paper fasteners
pushpins
rubber bands
ruler
stapler

Tyvek envelopes
yardstick

From Your Kitchen
½-gallon beverage cartons (e.g.,
milk, lemonade, or juice)
bamboo skewers
can with plastic lid
cardboard oatmeal container
cereal boxes
chopsticks
cookie tray
cornstarch
dried beans
flour
foam (e.g., meat tray, egg carton
top, plate, clamshell; see glossary
for full explanation)
foil pie pan
funnel
juice boxes
mini marshmallows
paper bowls
paper cups
paper plates
paper towel tubes
paper towels
plastic drinking straws (flexible
and regular)
plastic food storage containers
and lids (various sizes)
plastic knife
plastic soda bottles

plastic take-out containers with
lids
plates (6-inch, 8-inch, and 10-inch)
popcorn kernels
rice
rolling pin
toothpicks
twist ties
wax paper cereal bag
wine corks

From Your Laundry Room

clothespins (wooden, hinge type)
dry cleaner hangers (with
cardboard tube across bottom)
iron
old socks
old T-shirts
old white sheets
panty hose
wire hangers

From Your Party Supplies

balloons (party and water-balloon
size)
ribbon

tissue paper
wrapping paper tubes

From Your Toolbox

hammer
metal washers or nuts
nail
screw-in hook
thin dowel rod
utility knife (box cutter or X-Acto
knife)
wire cutters

Miscellaneous

cardboard boxes (shoe boxes
and small, medium, and large
corrugated cardboard boxes)
magazines
marbles
newspaper
photos
Ping-Pong ball
plastic eggs
spring rod for curtains
string

BALLOON PROJECTS

WHO DOESN'T LOVE a balloon? From tiny water balloons to giant hot-air balloons, floating helium balloons on strings, or long balloons twisted into creatures by clowns, balloons have many incarnations, but as the following toys show, balloons can be so much more than bags of hot air.

FACTS ABOUT BALLOONS

◆ Early balloons were made from dried animal bladders (yep, your bladder is where pee comes from).

◆ The rubber balloon was invented in 1824 by a scientist named Michael Faraday for experiments he wanted to do with different kinds of gases. He's also the guy who invented the electric motor. (Smart dude.)

◆ In the 1800s, you could buy a rubber balloon for a penny at the circus.

◆ Most party balloons are now made from latex, which comes from rubber trees. So you could say balloons come from trees.

◆ Helium balloons stop floating because the helium atoms escape through tiny holes, called pores, in the latex.

◆ About one billion balloons are set free each year.

◆ The balloons that are formed into different shapes such as poodles and swords are made of stretchier rubber than party balloons so they won't break when they're twisted and tied.

◆ Special balloons are used for a kind of surgery called angioplasty, when a doctor inserts a small balloon into a blood vessel that needs to be cleared.

Bobble-Head Balloons

Quick, easy, and fun. What could be better for your first homemade toy?

MATERIALS

small balloon (such as a water balloon) ▪ drinking straw
▪ transparent tape ▪ permanent markers

 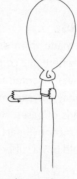

Blow up and tie a balloon then pull the loose end (below the knot) over one end of the straw.

Secure by winding a long piece of transparent tape around both the straw and the end of the balloon.

Draw a goofy face on the balloon.

EXTRA FUN

◆ Make lots of bobble heads to look like your friends, family, or favorite celebrities.
◆ Put on a bobble-head puppet show.
◆ Get crafty and add extra straws or chenille stems for arms and legs, then dress your creations with construction paper clothes.

Bobble heads have been around since the 1840s, but they didn't become popular until the 1960s, when Major League Baseball used them as team souvenirs.

Balloon Barbershop

Give your balloon bangs, a Mohawk, or a nice clean shave in a home salon.

MATERIALS

poster board or thin cardboard from a cereal box ▪ permanent markers ▪ balloon ▪ yarn ▪ transparent tape ▪ shaving cream ▪ plastic knife ▪ damp cloth or paper towel

Cut out and decorate a pair of 12-inch shoes from a piece of poster board or thin cardboard. Then cut a slit from the heels to the center of the feet.

Blow up and tie a large balloon then slip the knot of the balloon into the slit in the feet so the balloon stands up.

Draw a goofy face on the balloon with markers. Tape long pieces of yarn to the top of the balloon to make hair. Cut and style your balloon's hair.

Spread shaving cream over the cheeks and chin of the balloon and shave the customer with the smooth edge of the plastic knife. Wipe knife clean with the damp cloth between strokes.

EXTRA FUN
♦ Save the shaving cream for last and make shaving cream pictures on the tabletop.

> **FUN FACT**
>
> *Some ancient cultures believed good and bad spirits entered a person's body through the hair. A good haircut and clean shave by a barber was one way to get rid of bad spirits.*

Mini-Marshmallow Popper

WARNING: Whatever you do, do not pop marshmallows at other people. This would be a terrible thing to do. If you don't believe me, I'll tell you the story of the little boy with a pink marshmallow for an eye.

MATERIALS
paper cup ▪ scissors ▪ balloon ▪ rubber band ▪ mini marshmallows

Cut the bottom out of the cup so you have a big hole.

Without blowing up the balloon, tie a knot in the end, then snip off the top ½ inch of the balloon.

Stretch the balloon over the bottom of the cup so that the knot is in the center of the hole, then secure it with a rubber band around the cup.

Insert a mini marshmallow into the opening and gently shake the cup until the marshmallow snuggles down in the center of the balloon.

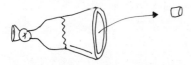

Face the popper away from you, and away from other people, then pull the knot back and let go. Watch your marshmallow zing through the air!

EXTRA FUN

- ◆ Try popping other soft things such as foam earplugs, cotton balls, wads of paper, etc.
- ◆ Make one for a friend then have a contest to see who can pop more marshmallows into a bowl a few feet away or whose can go the farthest.

> **FUN FACT**
>
> *Marshmallows were originally made by the Egyptians. They mixed honey with the sap of a plant called a marsh mallow. Now they're made from sweeteners like corn syrup and thickeners such as gelatin.*

Balloon Balls

These are great for juggling, playing catch, or squeezing when you're stressed because you can't learn to juggle.

MATERIALS

funnel ▪ four balloons (two different colors are nice) ▪ 1 cup cornstarch ▪ chopstick ▪ scissors

Place the funnel in the mouthpiece of one balloon. Pour cornstarch into the funnel and work it down into the balloon with the chopstick. Continue this until the body of the balloon is filled with cornstarch.

Cut half the mouthpiece (the curled lip) off the balloon, taking care not to spill the cornstarch.

Cut the entire mouthpiece off the other three balloons. Stretch one balloon over the filled one, making sure the open end is opposite the open end of the first balloon.

Do this twice more with the remaining two balloons (so the open end is always opposite the one beneath it) until you have a small, compact, two-colored ball.

◆ Play catch with a friend.
◆ Make more balloon balls and learn to juggle.

FUN FACT

In medieval Europe, court jesters sang, joked, and juggled to keep kings and queens entertained and healthy. Laughter was thought to dispel "black bile" in the body, which caused melancholia, or unhappiness.

Punch Ball

No need to wait for the next carnival to get a balloon punch ball. You will, however, have to wait if you want an elephant ear and a giant stuffed purple teddy bear.

MATERIALS

rice ▪ large balloon (the bigger and rounder the better)
▪ large rubber bands

Pour a tablespoon of rice into the balloon. (If you have trouble getting the rice in the balloon use a small funnel or roll up a small piece of paper and insert it into the balloon opening like a funnel.)

Blow the balloon up. Begin tying a knot, pausing before you pull the end of the balloon through the hole. Slip a rubber band through the hole, loop it over itself, then finish tying the knot.

Loop additional rubber bands to the first one to make a long handle.

Hold the free end of the rubber band then swing and punch the balloon while the rice sizzles away.

EXTRA FUN
- ◆ Join extra rubber bands together for a longer tether.
- ◆ Decorate the balloon with permanent markers.

Hot-Air Balloon

A simple hook in the doorway will take your balloon up, up, and away.

MATERIALS
balloon ▪ string ▪ scissors ▪ transparent tape ▪ hole punch
▪ small round food container (such as a yogurt cup) or a berry basket
▪ screw-in hook ▪ short stick (such as a chopstick or twig)

Blow up the balloon and tie it.

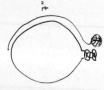

Measure a piece of string from the knot of the balloon to the top of the balloon then make the string four times this length. Make another string the same length.

$7" \times 4 = 28"$

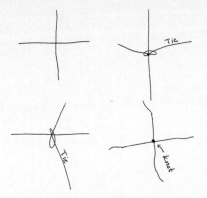

Lay the two long strings on the ground perpendicular to one another and crossing (so it looks like a plus sign).

Take the ends of one of the strings and tie them in a knot over the other string. Then tie the second string in a knot over the first string.

Lay the knot on top of the balloon and let the four strings drape evenly over the sides. Secure the top with a small piece of transparent tape. Now gather the string ends tightly at the knot of the balloon. Hold three strings securely while you wind the other string around the knot once then tie it, letting the long end dangle. Repeat with each string until all four strings are tied around the knot of the balloon. Finally, secure each string against the side of the balloon with a piece of transparent tape.

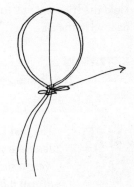

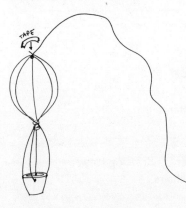

Punch four holes evenly around the sides of the small round container or berry basket. This will be the basket of the balloon.

Tie one string through each of the holes so the basket hangs evenly under the balloon.

Screw the hook into the top of a doorway.

Slip a piece of string under the knot on top of the balloon and tie. With the balloon basket resting on the floor, loop the string over the hook and let the loose end fall to the floor. Cut the string where it meets the floor, then tie the end around a stick.

Hold the stick and pull to lift the balloon in the air.

EXTRA FUN

◆ Take the clothespin people (page 60) for a ride.

FUN FACT

The first hot-air balloon was launched by French scientist Jean-Francois Pilatre de Rozier in 1783. The passengers were a sheep, a duck, and a rooster. The ride lasted fifteen minutes then crashed.

Zip-Line Balloon Racer

Ladies and gentlemen, start your, er, um, balloons!

MATERIALS

transparent tape ▪ balloon ▪ ruler ▪ drinking straw ▪ string ▪ scissors ▪ two kitchen chairs

To Make the Balloon Racer

Cut a piece of tape that's 1 inch shorter than
your deflated balloon.

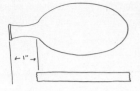

Fold the tape lengthwise, with the sticky side
facing out, to make a long, skinny tape loop.

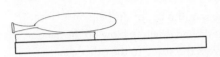

Line up one end of the tape loop
with one end of the straw, then
press the tape along the length of
the straw. (Don't worry, it'll only
cover a few inches.)

Position the balloon over the tape and straw so that the end of the
mouthpiece will hang over the end of the straw and the body of the balloon
will be attached to the straw. Press the balloon down to affix it.

Take a 2-inch piece of tape and
affix it loosely around the straw
and balloon near the mouthpiece.
This tape does two things: (1) It helps hold the balloon in place and (2) it
helps release the air more slowly when you're ready to make your balloon
racer zip. Don't make the tape too tight, or you won't be able to blow up
the balloon, but also, don't make it too loose, or you won't provide any
resistance for the air when you let the racer go.

Now your balloon racer is ready for the zip line.

To Make the Zip Line

Cut a 7-foot piece of string. Tie the string to the top of one chair, then slip the
straw of the balloon racer over the loose end of the string. Tie the loose end of
the string to the other chair. Pull the chairs apart until the string is taut.

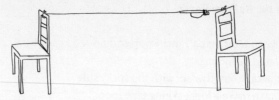

To Play

Position the balloon racer so that the mouthpiece of the balloon is close to one chair. Hold the racer steady and bend down to blow up the balloon. Release the racer and watch it zip across the string to the other chair.

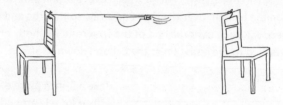

EXTRA FUN

◆ Measure how far your balloon racer goes with one puff of air, two puffs, three, etc.

◆ How many puffs does it take to get the balloon to the end?

◆ Set up two racers, side by side. Each player gets the same number of puffs into the balloon. Let go and watch them race.

◆ Make a longer zip line for more racing fun or try different shapes and sizes of balloons.

> **FUN FACT** *Balloon racers work because air rushes out of the open mouth of the balloon (this is called thrust) and pushes the balloon forward. This is an example of Isaac Newton's Third Law of Motion: For every action there is an equal and opposite reaction. It's the same reason rockets fly.*

CARDBOARD TUBE PROJECTS

CARDBOARD TUBES MIGHT win the award for most ubiquitous yet unappreciated resources in our lives. Toilet paper, paper towels, wrapping paper, and poster mailers all use this simple, yet versatile technology. Give your humble leftover tubes the chance for a second life with these projects.

FACTS ABOUT CARDBOARD TUBES

- In 1877, Seth Wheeler sold the first perforated toilet paper on a roll. Before people used paper to wipe their bums, they used things like corncobs, leaves, and rags, or lace if they were French kings and queens.
- Americans spend more money per year on toilet paper than any other country.
- Scott Paper Company invented paper towels by accident when a shipment of rolled paper was too thick for toilet tissue. The Scotts perforated the roll into towel-sized sheets and sold them as disposable "Sani-Towels" for use in public restrooms.
- Shigeru Ban, a Japanese architect, designs structures using recycled cardboard tubes to house disaster victims.
- **Question:** Why did the toilet paper roll down the hill? **Answer:** To get to the bottom.

Goofy Glasses with Fake Eyes

You can't hide those lying eyes, but no one will guess it's you stealing cookies from the cupboard if you slip on these glasses.

MATERIALS

toilet paper tube ▪ ruler ▪ markers ▪ scissors ▪ tracing paper ▪ two flexible drinking straws ▪ transparent tape ▪ stapler

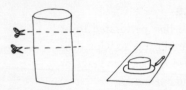

Cut two 1-inch segments from a toilet paper tube. Next, trace the rings onto a piece of tracing paper to make eye circles, leaving some space between them.

Draw four tabs coming out of the top, bottom, and each side of the eye circles. Use markers to draw funny eyes inside the circles then cut out the circles with their tabs.

Trim the two flexible straws so that they're the right length for the flexible tip to wrap around your ear and the rest of the straw to reach your temple.

Place the circles over the holes in the cardboard rings and fold the tabs over, then secure with tape. Staple the nonflexible end of one straw to the outside edge of each eye ring.

Use a 2-inch piece of a straw to make the nose piece by bending the sides down and stapling it to the inside edge of each ring. Wrap the flexible tips of the straws over your ears and see what funny looks you get.

EXTRA FUN

◆ Make glasses with different kinds of eyes. A fake mustache is always nice, too.

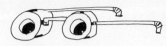

A person with two different-colored eyes has a condition called heterochromia iridum.

Indoor Tennis, Anyone?

You can play singles, doubles, or practice hitting on your own with this quick and easy tennis set.

MATERIALS

paper towel tube ▪ heavy-duty paper plate (or four flimsy ones, stacked and stapled together around the edges) ▪ masking tape ▪ markers (optional) ▪ rice ▪ balloon

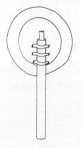

To make the racket, lay the paper towel tube on the back of the plate. Put a long strip of masking tape halfway into the tube with the rest attached to the back of the plate. Then, place long strips of tape across the tube and onto the plate.

Decorate the racket with markers if you want.

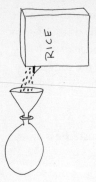

Drop a tablespoon of rice into the opening of the balloon. (This does two things: It makes a sizzly noise and gives the balloon some weight. If you have trouble getting the rice inside, you can make a simple funnel by rolling up a small piece of paper and inserting it partway into the opening.) Blow up the balloon and tie a knot.

See how many times you can hit the balloon before it touches the ground.

EXTRA FUN

◆ Make another racket for a friend. Then tie a jump rope between the backs of two chairs and cover with a sheet for a net. Hit the balloon back and forth over the net.

◆ If you make four rackets you can play doubles, which means two people play on each team.

FUN FACT

Tennis was first played by European monks during religious ceremonies. A few hundred years later, when the French royal family started playing, they yelled, "Tenez!" before they hit the ball, which means "play."

Kaleidoscope

Sparkly treasures make this kaleidoscope shine.

MATERIALS

mirror board (or cereal cardboard covered with foil)* ▪ ruler
▪ scissors ▪ toilet paper tube ▪ balloon ▪ large metal paper
clip ▪ transparent tape ▪ see-through plastic lid (at least twice
the circumference of the cardboard tube) ▪ white glue
▪ colorful plastic beads and sequins

* Note: If you can't find mirror board, you can make your own by gluing aluminum foil onto strips of cereal box cardboard. See instructions below for the correct measurements, then use a glue stick to cover one side of a cardboard strip and lay it on top of a larger piece of smooth aluminum foil. Now cover the exposed side of the cardboard strip with more glue. Fold the loose foil to cover the cardboard, and trim off the excess. Repeat to make the other two pieces.

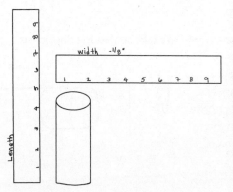

First you will make three strips of mirror board that will fit inside the cardboard tube. To get the correct dimensions, measure the diameter of the tube (that's the distance across the circle) and subtract ⅛ inch. This will be the width of each strip.

Next, measure the length of the cardboard tube. This will be the length of each strip.

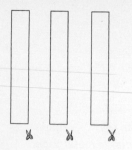

Now cut three strips of the mirror board using those dimensions.

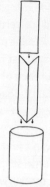

Insert the mirror board strips into the tube so they form a triangle.

Snip off a very itty-bitty tip of the balloon to make a tiny hole. Also cut off the mouthpiece (the curled lip).

Stretch the balloon mouth over one end of the tube so that the tiny hole is centered over the end.

Straighten out a large metal paper clip. Slip one end under the balloon and let the other end extend off the opposite end of the tube. Secure the clip to the top of the tube with transparent tape.

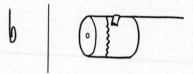

Dot the see-through lid with white glue and place colorful beads and sequins on top, then let the glue dry. Set one bead aside for later.

Once the beads and sequins are firmly in place, poke a tiny hole in the center of the lid, then slip the lid over the paper clip (the sparkly things should face away from the end of the tube). Place the leftover bead over the straightened paper clip and curl the end of the paper clip under so it's not poking out.

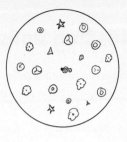

Look through the hole in the balloon, point the kaleidoscope toward the light, and spin the lid.

EXTRA FUN

- ◆ Decorate the outside of the kaleidoscope with construction paper, markers, or stickers.
- ◆ Make different lids to attach to the kaleidoscope.

FUN FACT

A Scottish scientist, Sir David Brewster, made the first kaleidoscope. He named his invention using two Greek words that together mean "beautiful form watcher."

Nesting Dolls

The first nesting dolls, called **matryoshka,** *were hand-carved out of wood in Sergiev Posad, Russia, but you can make your own with cardboard tubes and scissors.*

MATERIALS
wrapping paper tube ▪ scissors ▪ stapler ▪ markers ▪ transparent tape

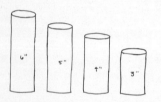

Decide how tall you want the first doll to be and cut that length from the wrapping paper tube, then cut three more lengths from the tube, each 1 inch shorter than the last. For example, if the first doll is 6 inches tall, the next will be 5 inches, the next 4 inches, and the last 3 inches.

Cut an opening up the back of the three smaller tubes (do not cut the biggest one). Working your way down the scale, trim the back seam in ¼-inch increments (¼ inch off the second doll, ½ inch off the third, ¾ inch off the fourth).

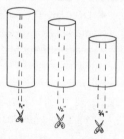

Staple or tape the seams of each tube so the tube will fit inside the next largest one, until you've gotten to the smallest, which will nest inside all the tubes.

Decorate the dolls with the markers. You might like to make a set of characters from a fairy tale (like the big bad wolf and the three little pigs, or Goldilocks and the three bears) or just draw faces on them. Nest the tubes all together.

EXTRA FUN

◆ Make a larger set of six or eight dolls.
◆ Cut the faces of your family out of photos and attach them to make a nesting family.

Pull-Along Snake or Millipede

Take your pick: creepy reptile or crawly bug.

MATERIALS
toilet paper tubes ▪ scissors ▪ ruler ▪ hole punch ▪ markers ▪ small paper clips ▪ string ▪ twist ties ▪ transparent tape

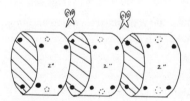

Cut several toilet paper rolls into 2-inch segments. Punch eight holes in each segment, four in the front (two on top and two on bottom) and four in the back (two on top and two on bottom).

Color each segment to look like a snake and draw a face on the first piece.

Join the segments together by lacing the paper clips into the holes you punched.

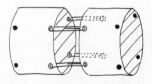

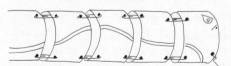

Punch a hole on the bottom of the first piece. Attach a long string. Pull your snake around.

If you want to make a millipede, take two long twist ties per section and fold them into wide M shapes, which will become the feet.

Attach the twist-tie feet with tape along the bottom at the front and back of each segment of the snake.

Tug on the string and watch your millipede skitter across the floor.

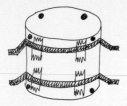

The word **millipede** *means "one thousand feet," but most millipedes have somewhere between 36 and 450 legs.*

Talking Finger Puppet

Unlike most finger puppets that just sit there . . . on your finger . . . doing nothing, this one has a mouth that moves. I wonder what it will say?

MATERIALS

toilet paper tube ▪ marker ▪ ruler ▪ scissors ▪ masking tape ▪ construction paper ▪ googly eyes, yarn, and/or chenille stems (optional) ▪ glue

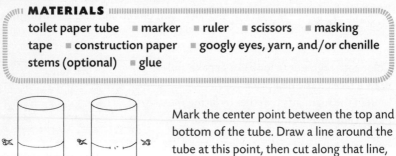

Mark the center point between the top and bottom of the tube. Draw a line around the tube at this point, then cut along that line, leaving 1 inch of the tube intact. (This will make a hinge for the puppet's mouth.)

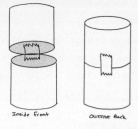

Inside Front   Outside Back

Reinforce the hinge with a strip of masking tape inside the tube and out.

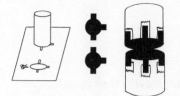

For the inside of the mouth, trace one end of the tube twice on a piece of construction paper, leaving some space between them. Draw three tabs sticking out from these circles, then cut the tabbed circles out.

Place the circles with tabs over the top and bottom openings of the mouth. Fold the tabs down and secure with transparent tape.

Cut two pieces of construction paper so they will wrap around the top and bottom of the tube. Secure with transparent tape on the back of the puppet.

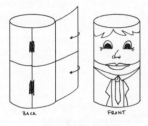

BACK   FRONT

Next draw and decorate a head on the top half (above the mouth) and a body on the bottom (below the mouth). This is a great time for googly eyes, yarn hair, chenille stem arms, or just crayons and markers if you want to make life less messy.

Cut two 1 x 3 inch strips of construction paper and form them into loops slightly bigger than the circumference of your pointer finger. Attach one loop to the back of the puppet just above the mouth hinge and one below. (If you have a long, skinny stapler that can reach down the tube, this works well, but you can also attach with transparent tape.)

Slip both loops over your pointer finger so that the puppet rests on the back of your hand (rather than on the palm side). Wiggle your finger to open and close the puppet's mouth.

EXTRA FUN

◆ Make more puppets. Have a conversation. Put on a show.

Ventriloquists can talk without moving their mouths. Most ventriloquists have a puppet, or "dummy," that they make talk in order to entertain people, but the first Greek ventriloquists were part of religious ceremonies and were called "stomach talkers." It was thought that the spirits of dead people went inside the ventriloquist's stomach and spoke through him.

Trombone

Like with a real trombone, moving the neck back and forth will make different notes in this cardboard version of the big brass horn.

MATERIALS

heavy-duty paper bowl ▪ two long cardboard tubes (one slightly larger than the other)* ▪ pencil ▪ ruler ▪ utility knife ▪ masking tape

* Note: One tube has to fit inside the other and slide easily; for example, a small mailing tube and a paper towel tube would work. If

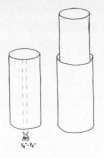

you can't find two different tubes, you could use two paper towel tubes. Cut down the back of one, lengthwise, and trim ⅛ inch off along the cut edge, then tape the seam back up.

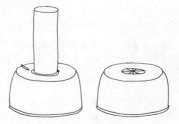

Turn the bowl upside down. Stand the larger of the tubes on the bowl and trace around the circle.

Use the ruler to draw four straight lines, crossing in the center of the circle (so that it looks like an asterisk).

Cut along these lines with the utility knife. (Work slowly and carefully by cutting from the outer edge of the circle toward the center so you don't rip the bowl.)

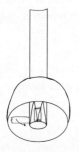

Gently push 2 inches of the larger tube through the cut circle. Turn the bowl over and look inside. You will see 2 inches of the tube poking through with points from the cut circle surrounding the sides of the tube. Place masking tape over each point, then over the top of the tube, and secure it to the inside of the tube. Once all the points have been taped, run a long piece of tape around the perimeter of the tube to secure everything.

Place the smaller tube inside the larger one.

To play your trombone, face the bowl away from you and the tubes near your mouth. Hold the top of the smaller tube with one hand and the base of the larger tube with the other. Press your mouth against the hole in the smaller tube and

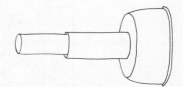

make a raspberry sound. Slide the tubes apart to bend the sound. Sing a melody while puttering your lips and moving the tubes to play a song.

EXTRA FUN

◆ Make all the musical instruments in this book with your friends and form your own band.

> **FUN FACT**
>
> *Trombones have been around for six hundred years. They were first called sackbuts. (And no, you may not call your brother a sackbut.)*

Tubular Drums

Drums are membranophones because they have a membrane, or head, stretched across the body. Different-sized cardboard tubes create different sounds in this tubular little drum set.

MATERIALS

six cardboard tubes of varying sizes (wrapping paper, paper towel, toilet paper) ▪ scissors ▪ ruler ▪ Tyvek envelope ▪ marker ▪ transparent tape ▪ rubber bands

Cut the tubes so you have segments that are 12, 10, 8, 6, 4, and 2 inches long.

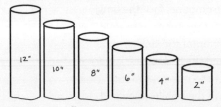

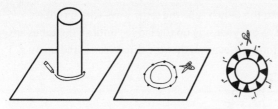

Cut out a large piece of the Tyvek envelope. Place one tube on top of the Tyvek and use a marker to draw a circle around the perimeter. To make the drumhead, draw another circle, 1 inch around the outside of the first. (Don't sweat this one. It doesn't have to be perfect. If you're doing it freehand, you can use a ruler to measure out 1 inch from the first circle, in eight different directions, making a dot each time. Connect these dots to draw the outside circle.)

Cut around the outside circle; then, every inch around the perimeter, cut a small triangular notch that extends to the original circle you drew.

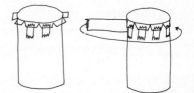

Put the head on top of the tube, lining up the original circle with the rim. Pull down each tab and secure with a small piece of tape. Do this all the way around the container. (Hint: Tape down a tab, then do the one opposite, so you can pull the head taut. Continue in this way until all tabs are taped down.) When the tabs are all taped down, run one long piece of tape around the perimeter of the tube to secure all the tabs.

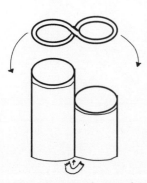

Repeat for each tube.

Connect the tubes with rubber bands. Start with the 2-inch and 4-inch tubes. Place them side by side so the bottoms are even. Hold them together by pinching the inside bottom walls together. Twist a rubber band into a figure 8. Put one loop over the 2-inch tube and the other loop over the 4-inch tube.

Secure the bottoms of these two tubes together with transparent tape.

Attach these two drums to the 6-inch tube the same way—with a rubber band and a piece of tape. Work your way up the ladder, until all the tubes are connected and their bottoms are even so that the drums can stand up on a flat surface.

Use a couple of sticks (such as chopsticks or unsharpened pencils) or rubber band and pencil mallets (page 144) to play the Tyvek heads. Notice how different-sized tubes make different tones.

EXTRA FUN

◆ Make all the musical instruments in this book with your friends and form your own band.

FUN FACT

*The word **tubular** used to be surfer slang for "awesome," because waves form tubes when they crest.*

CARDBOARD BOX PROJECTS

CARDBOARD BOXES COME in nearly every size imaginable, from the smallest jewelry box to humongous containers for appliances and giant TVs. They can be made from flimsy paperboard, such as cereal boxes, or heavy corrugated cardboard like the ones movers use. The heavier the cardboard, the trickier it is to cut, but also, the more interesting projects you can make.

FACTS ABOUT CARDBOARD BOXES

◆ Cardboard is made from layers of paper glued together.

◆ Silk merchants used cardboard boxes as early as 1840 for carrying *Bombyx mori* moths and their eggs from Japan to Europe.

◆ You can visit the Museum of the Cardboard Box (Musée du Cartonnage et de l'Imprimerie) in Valréas, France.

◆ The first American cardboard box was made in 1895.

◆ Before it was used in boxes, corrugated paper was used for the sweatbands in stovepipe hats, like the one Abraham Lincoln wore.

◆ In 2005, the cardboard box was added to the National Toy Hall of Fame.

Tips for Working with Cardboard Boxes

Anatomy of a Box

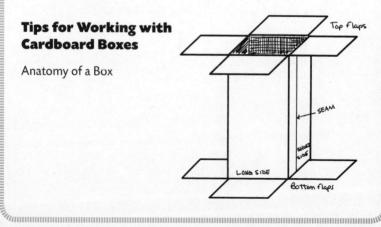

How to Cut Cardboard

1. For flimsy cardboard such as cereal boxes, use strong, sharp scissors that are the right size for your hand.
2. When you want to cut a straight line, first draw it on the cardboard using a ruler or yardstick, then cut along the line.
3. Use a utility knife to cut heavier corrugated cardboard (like big cardboard boxes). Remember: Utility knives are *very* sharp and should only be handled by adults.
4. When you want to cut a straight line on corrugated cardboard, lay the ruler or yardstick down and hold it firmly with one hand (making sure your fingertips are out of the way) while you run the utility knife along its edge.
5. Sometimes you'll want to fold a piece of cardboard back (for example, to make doors and windows that open and close). To do this, first draw a line with a ruler or yardstick, then score along the line with one leg of the scissors or the small, sharp tip of the utility knife. (To score means to cut lightly, only halfway through the cardboard, not all the way through.)
6. Circles are tricky to cut out of cardboard. First trace a circular object, such as a lid or plate, onto the cardboard. Then use the small sharp tip of the utility knife to cut around the circle. Work slowly in sections, turning the cardboard as you go.

Box Barn with Cork Horses

This simple structure makes a cozy home for sweet cork horses.

MATERIALS FOR THE BARN

small- to medium-sized corrugated cardboard box* ■ 3-inch-wide masking tape ■ pencil ■ ruler or yardstick ■ utility knife

* Note: Please read "Tips for Working with Cardboard Boxes" (pages 29–30) before you begin.

Open the top of the box so that four flaps hang down. You should have two large flaps and two small flaps.

Fold the two large flaps up so they meet at a peak above the box. Secure the peak with masking tape.

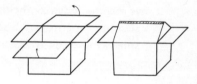

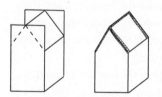

Fold each small flap up to meet the roof peak, then trace the triangular peak onto the inside surfaces of the small flaps. Use the utility knife and ruler to cut along the lines you've drawn. Your small flaps should now be triangular. Fold them up against the large-flap roof peak and secure with tape.

On the front of the barn, measure to the middle of the box. Draw large barn doors. Use the utility knife to cut the top, bottom, and center of the doors. Score the outside edge of each door so that it will open easily.

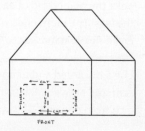

FRONT

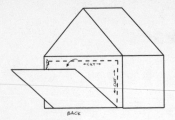

On the back of the box, draw straight lines 1 inch in from each side and the top. Use the ruler and utility knife to cut along those lines. When you're finished, you'll have a flap that opens in the back so you can reach inside the barn.

EXTRA FUN

- ◆ Use poster paint or markers to decorate your barn.
- ◆ Make craft stick corrals or oatmeal container silos to go with your barn.

MATERIALS FOR CORK HORSES

five round wooden toothpicks with pointed ends ▪ ruler ▪ scissors ▪ permanent black marker ▪ two wine corks ▪ glue ▪ small scrap of construction paper ▪ small scrap of yarn ▪ stapler

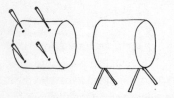

Cut two wooden toothpicks to 1½ inches long and two to 1¼ inches. (The longer toothpicks will be the front legs, and the shorter ones will be the back legs; this is so the weight of the head won't make the horse tip forward.)

Use the permanent marker to make dots where the legs will go on the bottom of one cork. The front legs should be about ¼ inch from the front of the cork and ½ inch apart. Same for the back legs on the other end. Carefully poke the pointy end of each toothpick into its mark at a slight angle to make the legs. The blunt ends will be the hooves. Test the body of the horse to make sure it stands up.

Use a discarded end of one toothpick to poke a hole in the top of the cork, centered between the front legs. Then poke a hole in the other cork about ¼ inch from one end. This will be the head.

Trim the remaining toothpick to 1 inch long for the neck. Carefully (because the toothpicks can break easily) insert the toothpick into the bottom of the head. Poke the other end of the toothpick neck into the hole on top of the body. Use the permanent marker to draw eyes and nostrils.

Glue small triangles cut from construction paper to the tiny discarded ends of the toothpicks. Stick them into the top of the head to make ears.

Cut two 2-inch pieces of brown yarn. Holding them together, tie a knot in the center. Fold the yarn over at the knot so you have four 1-inch strands. Place the knot on the top of the cork near the back and staple the yarn to the cork to make the tail.

FUN FACT

Corks are made from the bark of an oak tree found in Spain and Portugal.

Bigfoot Box Shoes

These giant shoes are great for silly dance parties or goofy relay races.

MATERIALS
two large empty shoe boxes ▪ utility knife ▪ glue ▪ masking tape ▪ paintbrush ▪ poster paint

Cut a semicircular hole in the center of the narrow side of the lid of one box. (The size of the hole will depend on the size of the wearer's feet. It should be big enough that the person can easily slip her feet into the opening, but not so big that her feet will come out when walking.)

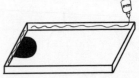

Line the inside rim of the box top with glue.

Put the lid on the box and secure with masking tape around the perimeter where the lid and box meet.

After this dries, decorate the box with poster paint to look like shoes (e.g., clown shoes or ballet shoes) or feet.

Repeat for the other foot.

- ◆ Have races while wearing the big feet. You can make a pair for each participant or have a relay race with two teams.
- ◆ Have a Monster Dance Party.

FUN FACT

Some people believe Bigfoot (a large, apelike creature that walks on two legs) lives in the forests of the U.S. Pacific Northwest, but no one has ever been able to prove its existence.

Cereal Box Façade Town

Eat your frosty flakes then turn the boxes and wax bags into bustling cities or quaint small towns.

MATERIALS

- cereal box
- (optional)
- cereal bag
- scissors
- ruler
- pencil
- utility knife
- markers, crayons, or magazine photos
- transparent tape
- white paper
- wax paper

Find the glued seam that runs along one side of the cereal box. Use your fingers to gently open the seam, then flatten out the box. Cut off the top and bottom flaps plus the front panel. What you have left is the back of the box as the center panel between two skinny sides.
Flip this over so the plain cardboard side faces up.

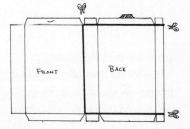

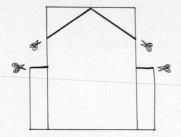

Trim the skinny side panels so they are half as tall as the center panel. Trim the top of the center panel into the shape of a roof (e.g., sloped roof, parapets, gabled roof, flat-topped skyscrapers.).

Use the ruler to sketch a door in the middle of the center panel. Cut up along the right vertical side of the door, then across the top. With the utility knife or one leg of the scissors, lightly score the left vertical side of the door.

Use the ruler to sketch the windows on the building then cut an I shape in them to mimic shutters. (You can do this with a utility knife, but before you cut, lay the building on top of a heavy piece of corrugated cardboard. Or you can use scissors by bending the box and snipping the center vertical line of each window, then bend the box the other way and snip across the top and bottom of each window.) Very lightly

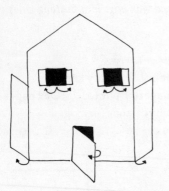

score the outside edges.

Decorate the building with markers, crayons, or collage photos from old magazines taped onto the cardboard. Fold the door open. Fold the shutters open. Fold the skinny sides back so your façade will stand upright.

To make stained-glass windows: Cut pieces of the wax paper cereal bag slightly larger than the windows. Decorate with permanent markers or crayons. Tape your stained-glass creations to the back of the windows.

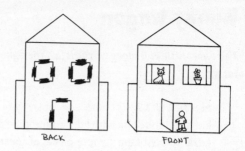

BACK   FRONT

To make surprises behind the windows: Attach white paper, instead of the wax paper, to the backs of the windows and the door. Open the shutters and the door to draw little scenes of what's going on inside your building.

EXTRA FUN

- ◆ Create clothespin people (see page 60) to populate your town.
- ◆ Make more façades with different styles of roofs, windows, and doors.
- ◆ Use toilet paper rolls to give the townsfolk chimneys, silos, and trees or make a castle with turrets for clothespin royalty.
- ◆ Create skyscrapers for a city look.

FUN FACT

Kellogg's was the first company to sell cereal in a cardboard box, in 1907. The first cereal box prize it offered was the "Stuff-Yourself Nursery Rhyme Ragdoll."

Bunny Wagon

This sweet little pull-along wagon is just the right size to take a favorite soft friend for a ride.

MATERIALS

kid-sized shoe box with lid ▪ wrapping paper ▪ scissors ▪ glue ▪ transparent tape ▪ four pieces of construction paper ▪ crayons or markers ▪ poster board ▪ ruler or yardstick ▪ glue stick ▪ two cotton balls or small pom-poms ▪ pushpin ▪ wire hanger ▪ wire cutters ▪ four identically sized plastic lids ▪ four or five jingle bells (optional) ▪ hole punch ▪ string

Take the lid off the shoe box. Wrap the shoe box and lid with wrapping paper, gluing down the edges and reinforcing them with tape. Set both aside to dry completely.

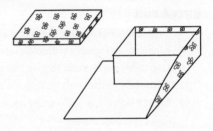

Draw a bunny (or trace the template on page 210) on one piece of 8 x 11 inch construction paper so that it will cover a long side of the box, then cut it out. Now trace it onto the other three pieces of paper and cut these out, too.

Draw a line across the poster board 1 inch from the bottom edge. First, glue a bunny onto the poster board so that it's sitting on this line, leaving a 1-inch border at the

bottom. (This will slip inside the lid of the box so it won't be seen.) When the glue is dry, carefully cut out the bunny.

Flip the poster board bunny over and glue another bunny to the other side. Repeat with the remaining two bunnies. Color and decorate the bunnies so they all look the same. Finally, glue a cotton ball or pom-pom onto the outside back of each bunny to make a little fluffy tail.

Glue the bunnies so they are across from one another on the long sides of the shoe box. The bottom of the 1-inch border should be even with the bottom of the box. Set aside to dry.

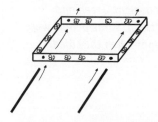

Turn the lid upside down and make a dot 2 inches from the back along the long side. Do the same on the other side and then the same from the front on both sides. Use a pushpin to poke a hole where the dots are. This will be the guide hole for the wire hanger axles that you will make next.

Use the wire cutters to cut the long base of a wire hanger into two equal lengths. Put one wire through each of the pairs of axle holes in the lid of the box.

Use the pushpin to poke a hole in the center of all four plastic lids. Slip the lids over the hangers on either side of the box. If you want the wagon to sing a happy tune, slip a jingle bell over the ends of the hangers. Use the tip of the wire cutters to curl the ends of the wires around so that the wheels are snug against the box.

Punch a hole in the center of the front edge of the box. Attach a long string. If you want more jingly fun, slip another bell over the string, then tie a knot.

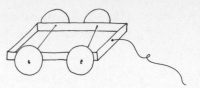

Now put the bunny box inside the lid and pull the wagon.

EXTRA FUN

◆ Design different critters for the sides of your wagon. Instead of gluing the bunny to the box, use four ½-inch pieces of self-adhesive hook-and-loop fastener on the poster board critter and the sides of the box, then swap out different critters.

Toy wagons go way back. Even ancient Greek and Egyptian children played with them. Some people were even buried with their toy wagons when they died.

Human Habitrail

The mole people are coming . . .

||||| **MATERIALS** ||||||||||||||||||||||||||||||||||||||||||||||||||||||||||||||||||||||
   three or more large cardboard boxes*   ■ pencil   ■ yardstick
   ■ utility knife   ■ craft glue (such as Gorilla Glue)   ■ duct tape

* Note: Please read "Tips for Working with Cardboard Boxes" (pages 29–30) before you begin.

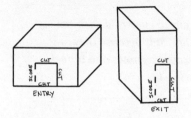

Decide which two boxes will be the starting and ending points, or anchor points, for the habitrail. The other box or boxes will be the connector tunnels. In one anchor box, use the yardstick to draw an entrance door. In the other anchor box, draw an exit door. Use the utility knife to cut the right side and top and bottoms of the doors, then lightly score the left side.

Arrange the other boxes between the anchors. (Stand some boxes up tall and lay others long and low.)

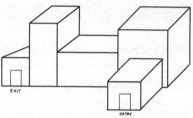

Cut slot-and-tab openings between the boxes to fit them together as shown below. Make sure the openings are large enough to crawl through. Glue and/or tape extra flaps to the inside of the boxes.

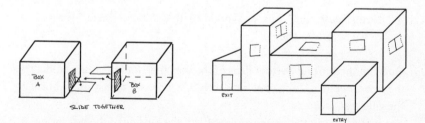

Last, cut windows in all the boxes to peek out while crawling through.

EXTRA FUN
♦ Put pillows, blankets, or stuffed animals inside.

◆ Decorate the inside and outside of the boxes with poster paint, markers, glow-in-the-dark stickers, or collages from magazine pictures.

People often set up habitrails to entertain their pet hamsters. Hamsters like habitrails because they are similar to the long, complicated burrows and tunnels hamsters in the wild dig to live in.

Castle with a Drawbridge

This is the perfect hideaway for princesses and knights.

MATERIALS

large corrugated cardboard box (e.g., from a refrigerator, range, or washing machine)* ▪ utility knife ▪ yardstick ▪ black permanent marker ▪ gray poster paint (optional) ▪ craft glue (such as Gorilla Glue) ▪ duct tape ▪ hole punch ▪ large paper clips

* Note: Please read "Tips for Working with Cardboard Boxes" (pages 29–30) before you begin.

Open up the top and bottom flaps of the box, then find the seam holding the sides together. Using your hand, carefully open up that seam by breaking the glue seal.

Lay the box out flat on the ground (with the outside of the box facing up—this will become the inside of your castle because it will likely have words printed on it). Cut off the top and bottom flaps.

Using your yardstick, sketch out then cut the parapets from the top as shown on the next page.

Sketch, then cut out the drawbridge door by cutting the top and both sides of the door then scoring across the bottom, 5 inches above the bottom of the box. This will allow the drawbridge door to fall open.

Work on the windows by sketching, then cutting out I shapes inside them and scoring along the sides to create shutters that open and close.

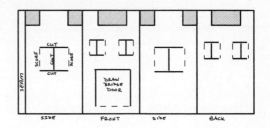

If you'd like to make your castle collapsible for easy storage, measure and mark the center point on the top and bottom of each side panel. Use your yardstick to draw a straight line down the middle of the side (this will transverse your window,

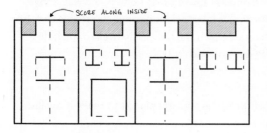

then score along this line with the utility knife. Do the same on the other side panel of the house. (Hint: Find a corrugated groove and use a light score; don't push too hard or you'll go all the way through.) Now the sides will fold in half easily.

If you'd like to decorate the castle, flip it over so the inside of the box is facing up. (This will be the outside of your castle since it's plain cardboard and can be decorated.) Draw bricks with your black permanent markers or get supercrafty and paint the entire thing gray, then add brickwork designs.

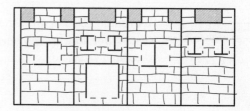

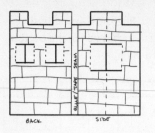

BACK   SIDE

Fold the box over on itself so the outside is facing up and reconnect the seam. Use strong craft glue and/or duct tape. Place heavy objects over the seam (such as books or bricks) until the seam is firmly reattached.

Once the glue dries, stand the castle up.

FRONT   SIDE

To finish the drawbridge door, punch a hole in the upper left and upper right corner of the door and also directly above those holes in the wall above the door. Make two long paper-clip chains and use them to attach the hole in the wall to the hole in the door on each side.

EXTRA FUN

◆ Decorate the interior of the castle and add pillows to make it royally comfy.
◆ Paint the door and window shutters to look like wood.
◆ Add vines and flowers up the sides.
◆ Use additional boxes to add more rooms to the castle.

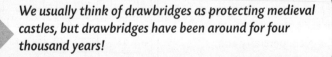

FUN FACT

We usually think of drawbridges as protecting medieval castles, but drawbridges have been around for four thousand years!

Collapsible Big Box Playhouse

This project is involved and a little tricky, but well worth it if you're short on space and need toys that can fold flat for storage. This playhouse can easily slip behind the couch when it's not popped open in the middle of the living room.

MATERIALS

two big cardboard boxes (washing machine or refrigerator boxes work well)* ▪ utility knife ▪ pencil ▪ yardstick ▪ paint (poster or wall paint) ▪ craft glue (such as Gorilla Glue) ▪ duct tape

* Note: Please read "Tips for Working with Cardboard Boxes" (pages 29–30) before you begin.

* Note: One box will become the house and one will become the roof. If you have two different-sized boxes, use the box with the lengthiest long side for the house.

Step 1: Prepare the Box for the House

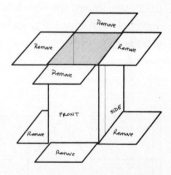

Cut off the top and bottom flaps from the box then stand it up and make sure it's sturdy. If not, trim the bottom until the box stands upright. Mark with your pencil which panels will be the front and back of the house and which will be the sides.

Open up the box by splitting the glued seam with your hand. You will have a thin flap of cardboard sticking out. It's important to keep this piece intact because you'll use it to reattach the sides of the box later on. Lay the box flat on a safe work surface with the inside (plain side) facing up.

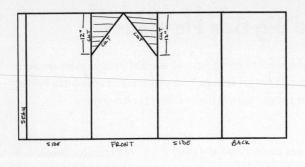

To make the peak of your house, mark the center point at the top of the front of the house. Next, mark a dot at the left and right edges of the front of the house 12 inches from the top. Use the yardstick to draw a straight, diagonal line from the left-edge dot to the center dot, then do the same from the right-side dot to the center dot. Hold the yardstick against one of these peak lines and cut with the utility knife. Cut the other peak line. Discard the extra pieces.

Fold the box so that the front panel of the house lies on top of the back panel. Trace the peak lines. Unfold the box then cut out the rear peak with your utility knife. Discard the extra pieces.

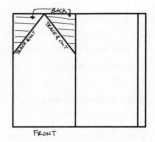

With the box lying flat and fully open, draw a line on both side panels connecting the bottoms of the peaks. Use your utility knife and yardstick to cut the side panels along these two lines. Keep these scraps to make shutters.

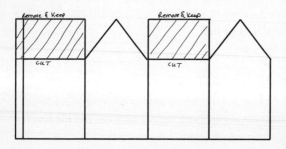

Measure and mark the top and both sides of the door on the front of the house. (The height depends on how big your box and its inhabitants are.) Use the utility knife to cut all the way through the top of the door and the right side. Lightly score the left side of the door so it will open and close easily.

Next, measure and mark windows on each side of the house, and draw an I shape inside each. Cut through the top, bottom, and center line of each window. To make shutters that open and close, score the left and right sides of the windows and fold the flaps back.

To make the house collapsible, measure and mark the center point at the top and bottom of each side panel. Use your yardstick to draw a straight line down the middle of the side (this will transverse your window). Score along this line from the top of the side panel to the top of the window, then from the bottom of the window to the bottom of the side panel. Do the same on the other side panel of the house. (Hint: Find a corrugated groove and use a light score; don't push too hard or you'll go all the way through.) Now the sides will fold in half easily.

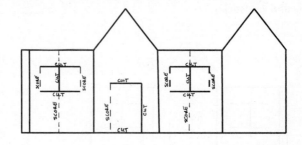

Step 2: Make the Roof

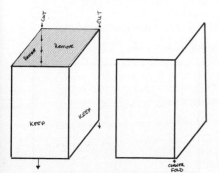

You will use two adjacent sides of the other box to make the roof. In order to do this, cut off the top and bottom flaps of the second box. Next, cut two corner seams of the box, opposite diagonally from one another so that what you have left is two sides of the box, still attached to one another by a corner fold. Set aside.

Measure the width of one side of the house (the distance between the front of the house and the back). Add 8 inches to this for an overhang. This is the length of your roof.

Lay the roof piece on the work surface with the corner fold perpendicular to you (so it runs left to right). (This seam will be the center of the roof and will lay between the front and back peaks of the house.)

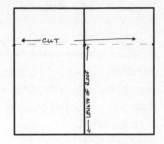

Measure the length of the roof along the corner fold and mark a dot. Do the same thing at each edge of the roof section. Draw a straight line across these three dots and cut using your utility knife and yardstick.

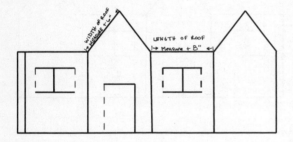

For the width of your roof, measure from the top of the house peak to the bottom and add 6 inches for an overhang.

On the roof piece, measure the width of the roof from the center seam out toward one edge and mark it with a dot. Do this at several points along the seam, then connect the dots and cut.

Do the same along the other side of the seam.

If the center seam does not fold easily, score it lightly on the outside of the roof.

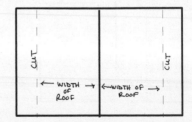

Step 3: Decorate

Flip the house over so that the outside of the house (which is the plain cardboard inside of your box) faces up. Paint walls and roof, then add details with paint or permanent markers.

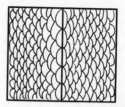

Step 4: Reattach the Sides of the House

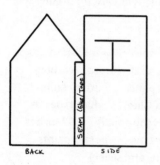

Once the decoration is dry, find the extra flap of cardboard from the seam you opened at the beginning of the project. Fold the entire box in half so that you can cover the inside of this seam with heavy-duty glue and reattach it to the outside of the box. (Note: You may need to score this seam so that it will fold nicely before you glue it.) Put some heavy books or weights on the seam until the glue dries. Reinforce the seam with duct tape. Touch up with paint.

Step 5: Put It All Together

Stand the house upright and place the roof on top with the center seam touching the peak of the front and back.

To collapse the house, remove the roof and fold in half. Gently

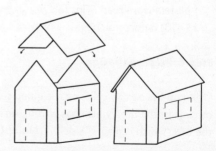

push the sides of the house in so the center wall seams fold. The house will accordion in on itself and be flat, with the front door facing forward.

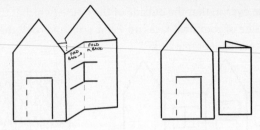

Rocket Ship

It may not be rocket science, but this project takes some time and patience. It'll be well worth it, though, when Buzz Aldrin and Sally Ride blast off to outer space right outside your back door.

MATERIALS

large corrugated cardboard box (such as a refrigerator, washing machine, or wardrobe moving box)* ▪ pencil ▪ utility knife ▪ yardstick ▪ craft glue (such as Gorilla Glue) ▪ duct tape ▪ glow-in-the-dark star and planet stickers (optional) ▪ 32 inches of self-adhesive hook-and-loop fastener tape ▪ poster paints (colors like black, white, red, orange, blue, and silver)

* Note: Please read "Tips for Working with Cardboard Boxes" (pages 29–30) before you begin.

Step 1: Prepare the Box

Open up the box by splitting the glued seam with your hand. Mark the outside of the box (which has writing on it) "Side 1." Mark the inside of the box (which is plain) "Side 2." (Note: The outside of the box, side 1, will become the inside of the rocket and vice versa.) Lay the box flat with side 2 facing up, on a safe cutting surface. Label the panels A, B, C, and D.

If your box has flaps on the top, cut them off, but leave the flaps on the bottom intact.

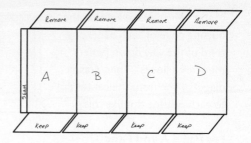

Step 2: Create the Top

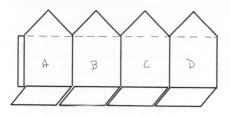

To make the top of the rocket, follow the detailed instructions below so that you cut the top third of each panel into a triangle shape.

Instructions

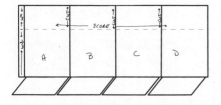

Measure the length of the box. Draw a line across the width of the panels that is one-third of the way down from the top. (For example, if your box is 48 inches long, your line will go across the box at 16 inches from the top.)

Using the utility knife, cut the seams between each panel starting at the top and ending at this line. Then, using your utility knife, score across the panels on the line you made. (This will make the triangular flaps fold easily.)

Now make the triangles. First, draw a dot at the center of the top of each panel. (For example, if the panel A is 24 inches wide, make a dot at 12 inches. Note: The panels may be different widths, so measure each one to find its center.) Next, make a dot at the outside edge of each panel one-third of the way down (where the scored line is). Then draw a diagonal line from the center dot to each outside dot like this:

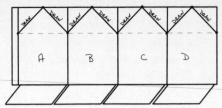

For Panel A and Panel C

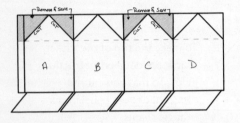

Hold your yardstick along one of the diagonal lines on panel A. Run the utility knife along the edge of the yardstick to cut through the cardboard. Do the same for the other diagonal line on panel A. Now the top of panel A will be shaped like a triangle. Set aside the smaller triangular pieces you cut off because you will use them later to create fins on the rocket. Repeat this process on panel C.

For Panel B and Panel D

On these panels you will create tabs that will make the peaks of the rocket stay together easily. First score the diagonal lines on panels B and D—do not cut all the way through.

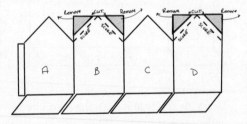

Next, draw a parallel line 2 inches outside of each line you just scored, then use the yardstick and utility knife to cut all the way through this line. Remove the triangular pieces you just cut off and set them aside for later.

Step 3: Make the Doors and Windows

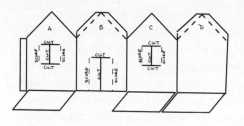

Cut off the bottom flap from panel B (but leave the flaps on panels A, C, and D to make fire later). Use the yardstick and pencil to draw a door on panel B that best fits the size of your rocket and the astronauts who will use it. For example, our box is 48 x 24 inches. The top 16 inches form the peak so we have 32 x 24 inches available for the door. We made a door 24 inches tall and 15 inches wide. Draw an I shape in the door. Cut along the top, center, and bottom of the door. Score the right and left sides.

Use the yardstick and pencil to draw windows on panels A and C, and draw an I shape in each. Cut the tops, centers, and bottoms with the utility knife. Score the right and left sides.

Step 4: Decorate the Inside (Optional)

If you want to decorate the inside of your rocket, flip the box over so side 1 faces up. Decorate it now, before you stand the box up and put the rocket together. Some ideas:

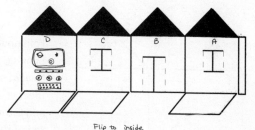

Flip to inside

Paint the inside black. When the paint is dry, attach glow-in-the-dark star and planet stickers to the top.

Use paint, markers, or construction paper to create control panels and windshields on the inside back panel.

Step 5: Put the Rocket Together

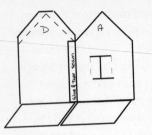

Once the paint on the inside is dry, keep the box on the floor and fold it so that panels A and D are on top and panels B and C are on the bottom. Cover the seam from panel A with heavy-duty glue and attach it to panel D. (Note: You may need to score this seam so that it will fold nicely before you glue it.) Put some heavy books or weights on the seam until the glue dries. Once it's dry, reinforce the seam with duct tape.

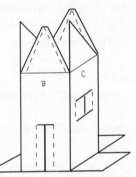

Now stand the box upright. Unfold the bottom flaps from panels A, C, and D so they lie flat against the floor on the outside of the box. This will help it stay upright and sturdy. (Plus, see next page for painting them to look like fire!)

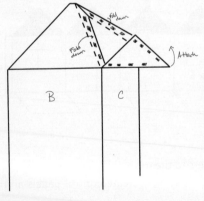

Fold down the tabs on the top of panels B and D then fold these panels toward one another until their peaks meet in the center. Fold panels A and C toward B and D to form the top of the rocket. Cut sixteen 2-inch strips of self-adhesive hook-and-loop fastener tape and attach four pieces evenly spaced across each tab. Attach the corresponding pieces to the inside edges of panels A and C. Press the panels together so the hook-and-loop fasteners meet. Now the peak of your rocket will stay together.

Step 6: Decorate the Outside

To make fins, attach the extra triangular pieces (the ones you cut off when making the rocket peaks) to the corners of the box using duct-tape hinges. For each fin:

1. Lay a triangle on the floor.
2. Cut a piece of duct tape the length of one edge.
3. Lay the duct tape lengthwise over this edge so that it is half-way on the cardboard and halfway off. Attach to the side of the box.

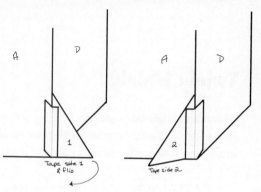

4. Fold the fin back and repeat with tape on the other side.

For extra coolness, sketch fire on the bottom flaps. Then use your utility knife to cut around the fire shape and paint it red and orange.

Finally, use paint, markers, stickers, and/or construction paper to decorate the outside of your rocket.

Step 7: Storing Your Rocket

When you come back from outer space, your rocket will fold down and slip inside a closet. Loosen the hook-and-loop fasteners to release the peaks, then fold the rocket flat, taking care to fold the fins and fire flaps, too.

EXTRA FUN

◆ Mini-marshmallow poppers (page 4) are the perfect alien defense system.

FUN FACT

The first rocket was probably a flying wooden pigeon toy made in Greece by a man named Archytas, in around 400 BC. The Russians launched the first rocket, called Sputnik, into outer space in 1957.

Twirly Whirly

Pioneer kids made these spinners with big wooden buttons on a string, but since most of us don't wear overcoats with giant wooden buttons anymore, save some scraps from your cardboard box projects to make these twirly whirlies.

MATERIALS

corrugated cardboard scraps ▪ yogurt cup ▪ pencil ▪ scissors ▪ hole punch ▪ four paper clips ▪ 1 yard of string

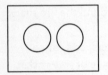

Use the yogurt cup as a template to draw two circles on the cardboard. Then cut the circles out.

Punch two holes on one piece of cardboard. Position them so that they are next to each other, on either side of the center. Lay the piece of cardboard with holes on top of the other. Mark the hole locations on the second piece, then punch the holes out of that circle as well.

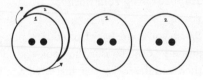

Put the two pieces together so that the holes line up. Fasten the pieces together with four paper clips spread evenly around the circle.

Slip one end of the string through one hole, then the other end through the remaining hole. Tie the ends together so you have a large loop going through the center of the cardboard circles.

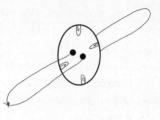

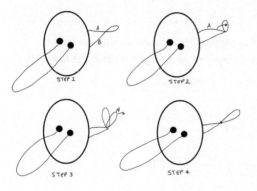

Pinch 2 inches of string on one end of the loop. Twist the loop and pull one piece of string through to create a knot with a finger loop at the end of the string. Do the same thing on the other end, making sure the string is even between the two finger loops.

Hold the finger loops and spin the cardboard disk until the string is twisted tightly, then pull and watch the twirly whirly whirl between your hands.

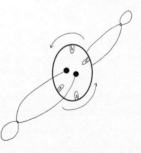

EXTRA FUN

- ◆ Try larger or smaller templates for the circles.
- ◆ Create new shapes for the twirly whirlies, such as a buzz saw or a flower.
- ◆ Decorate your twirly whirlies with markers and/or stickers.
- ◆ Use bright metallic paper clips for extra color.
- ◆ Add bells or beads to the ends of the paper clips.

Pioneer kids also played games such as hide-and-seek, hopscotch, hand clap games, and jump rope just like kids play today.

CLOTHESPIN PROJECTS

CLOTHESPINS MAY SEEM outdated if you're a fan of automatic dryers, but these ingenious little gadgets are as useful as ever when you're making toys. For these projects, I've used mostly wooden hinged clothespins, which are two-piece doohickeys with a small metal hinge between the legs. You might also find wooden slot clothespins, which are great for making clothespin people.

FACTS ABOUT CLOTHESPINS

◆ People probably carved their own wooden slot clothespins or bought them from peddlers who traveled the countryside until David M. Smith invented the first hinged clothespin in 1853.

◆ In 1976, sculptor Claes Oldenburg made a 45-foot-high clothespin sculpture that stands in Philadelphia.

◆ The Smithsonian's National Museum of American History in Washington, DC, had an exhibition called "American Clothespins" in 1998 that traced the history of the humble gadget.

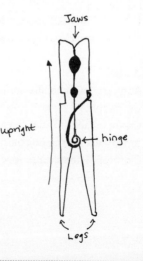

Anatomy of a Clothespin

Clothespin People

These fine folks are the perfect inhabitants for all sorts of make-believe places.

‖‖‖ **MATERIALS** ‖‖
clothespins* ▪ markers

* Note: Please see "Anatomy of a Clothespin" (page 59) before you begin.

You could use either the wooden slot or wooden hinge type of clothespin for this project. The slot version is straightforward—the head is the knob on top, the legs are the pegs on the bottom.

To use a wooden hinge–type clothespin face the clothespin upright, so the jaws are facing up and the legs are facing down, then turn it sideways so you can see both legs.

Use markers to draw a face above the hinge and clothing below the hinges.

EXTRA FUN

◆ Add yarn hair, chenille-stem arms, or fabric clothes to the people.
◆ Create inhabits for the cereal box façade town (page 35) or workers for the box barn with cork horses (page 31).
◆ Clothespin people also love to live in shoe boxes.

Clothespin Fairies

You'll get two for the price of one in this project, since each clothespin makes two dainty fairies.

MATERIALS

clothespin* ▪ permanent markers ▪ small scraps of yarn or string ▪ glue ▪ small piece of tissue paper ▪ chenille stem ▪ transparent tape

* Note: Please see "Anatomy of a Clothespin" (page 59) before you begin.

Give the legs of the clothespin a little twist and pop off the metal hinge that holds them together so you have two wooden halves. Discard the hinge, or better yet, put it in your craft box for another project another time.

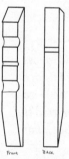

Front   Back

The inside of each clothespin leg (which has three grooves) will be the front of your fairy. The outside of the leg will have one groove about one-third of the way down from the top. This is the back of the fairy.

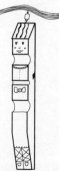

Use markers to draw a face at the top of the wooden piece and clothes down the body, ending with feet at the bottom of the piece.

To make hair, cut a few scraps of yarn and glue to the top part of the head, which is slightly sloped and flat.

To make wings, cut two long oval shapes from scraps of tissue paper (using two or more colors looks pretty). Put the layers together then pinch the middle and set aside.

To make the arms, cut a 4-inch length of chenille stem. Lay it across the groove on the back of the fairy so the arms are even. Lay the wings on top of the stem at the back and secure with tape.

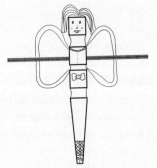

Do the same for the other wooden leg to make another fairy.

EXTRA FUN

- ◆ Give your fairies a ride on the fairy-go-round (page 161).
- ◆ Wooden clementine crates make excellent fairy homes.

FUN FACT

In 1920, photos that cousins Elsie Wright and Frances Griffith had taken of themselves playing with fairies in Elsie's garden became public. Many people believed the photos were real. Late in her life, Elsie admitted the fairies were not real. (She had drawn them.) But, that doesn't mean fairies don't exist.

Hungry Platypus

This funny little fellow waddles along looking for a snack to fill his clothespin snout.

⁘⁘⁘ **MATERIALS** ⁘⁘⁘⁘⁘⁘⁘⁘⁘⁘⁘⁘⁘⁘⁘⁘⁘⁘⁘⁘⁘⁘⁘⁘⁘⁘⁘⁘⁘⁘⁘⁘⁘⁘⁘⁘

clothespin* ▪ paper cup (big enough to fit your hand inside)
▪ pencil ▪ utility knife ▪ masking tape ▪ two balloons
▪ scissors ▪ masking tape ▪ permanent markers ▪ four jumbo
craft sticks

* Note: Please see "Anatomy of a Clothespin" (page 59) before you begin.

For this project, the clothespin will slip through a hole you make in the bottom of the cup. To make that hole, first turn the cup upside down. Place the clothespin against the rim that runs around the bottom, so that the pin is standing upright. With a pencil, trace around the sides of the clothespin legs.

Use your utility knife to carefully cut around the inside of the marks and the inside of the rim so the opening will be slightly smaller than the area covered by the legs of the clothespin.

Tear off three 1-inch pieces of masking tape to reinforce the edges of your cutout section. (Hint: Do the outside of the cup first, then turn the cup over and do the inside, smoothing down the tape with the eraser side of the pencil if you can't get your hand inside the cup.)

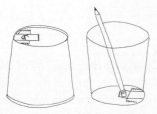

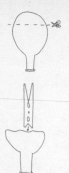

Cut off the top ¼ inch of one balloon. Slide the clothespin, jaw end first, into the balloon through the opening you just made. Push the clothespin into the balloon's mouthpiece so that the jaws of the clothespin come almost to the end of the mouthpiece and the legs of the clothespin stick out the other end of the balloon.

From the outside bottom of the cup, push the legs of the clothespin through the opening. Then stretch the balloon up and around the outside of the cup, pulling it as far as you can down the cup. (Depending on the size of the cup and the balloon, it will probably reach about halfway.) Now the mouthpiece of the balloon is sticking out of the bottom of the cup and you can reach inside the cup to open and close the pin. This is the duckbill of your hungry platypus.

Use permanent markers to draw eyes on the balloon above the balloon's mouthpiece.

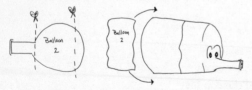

Cut the mouthpiece and the top ¼ inch off the other balloon so you have a large stretchy balloon band. Stretch this balloon band over the other end of the cup so that it covers any of the exposed cup. Overlap the ends of the balloons so the entire outside of the cup is covered but the cup opening remains uncovered. (If your cup is really long, you may need more balloons to cover the whole body.)

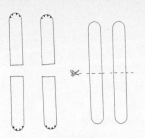

Cut both craft sticks in half. On the rounded end of each half, cut four small notches so that the ends resemble webbed feet.

Stick the front legs under the lip of the topmost balloon so they stick out beneath the face of the body. Stick the rear legs under the opposite end of the balloon so they stick out from the back of the body.

Reach your hand inside the cup and pinch the end of the clothespin to make the platypus's mouth move. Watch him trundle around looking for a tasty treat.

FUN FACT

Platypuses (and echidnas) are the only mammals that lay eggs instead of giving birth to live babies. A baby platypus is sometimes called a puggle.

Piano

Made from clothespins and jingle bells, this little piano rocks!

MATERIALS

12-inch-long chenille stem ■ thirteen pony beads ■ twelve clothespins* ■ paint and/or markers (optional) ■ large adult-sized shoe box ■ construction or wrapping paper (optional) ■ glue ■ thread ■ needle ■ twelve jingle bells ■ scissors ■ masking tape

* Note: Please see "Anatomy of a Clothespin" (page 59) before you begin.

Put a pony bead on one end of the chenille stem. Twist the stem to secure. Slip the long free end of the chenille stem through the hole of the metal hinge on the clothespin.

Add a bead, then another clothespin. Continue in this pattern (bead, pin, bead, pin . . .) until all twelve clothespins are on the stem, each separated by a bead. You

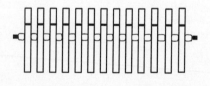

should end with the final pony bead. Twist the stem to secure the end. These are your piano keys. (If you want to paint them black and white to look like real piano keys, do so now and set them aside to dry.)

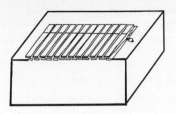

Remove the lid of the shoe box and discard. If you want to decorate the body of your piano, paint the box or cover it with construction or wrapping paper.

Put a line of glue on the bottom of each clothespin/piano key. Turn the box upside down. Place the "keys," glue side down, on the flat surface (which was the bottom) of the box so that the ends of the clothespins are even with the edge and the jaws of the clothespins face the center. Press down and let the glue dry.

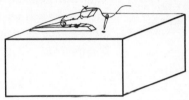

Cut a 12-inch length of thread. Press down on the first key to lift up the tip of the clothespin. Slip the thread under the tip so that it rests in the groove. Tie the thread securely around the top of the key.

Pull the long end of the thread through the eye of the needle. Pull the thread forward so it goes over the front end of the key. Poke the needle through the box in front of the key.

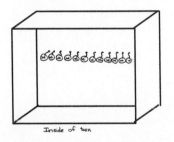

Inside of box

Turn the box over and pull the needle and thread through to the inside. Slip a bell over the needle and thread. Tie it securely about 1 to 2 inches from the hole. Trim the excess thread.

Flip the box back over. Trim any excess thread from the knot on top of the key. Make sure the thread is positioned over the front of the key and secure with a thin strip of tape.

Repeat this process to attach a bell to each key.

When all the keys have bells, turn the box over so the keys are on top and play!

EXTRA FUN

◆ Use bells of different shapes and sizes to get varying pitches.
◆ Make all the musical instruments in this book with your friends and form your own band.

FUN FACT

Wolfgang Amadeus Mozart began playing the clavier (a small instrument like the piano) when he was three. By the time he was seven, he amazed audiences (including kings and queens) by playing the piano backwards and blindfolded.

CRAFT STICK PROJECTS

I'M NOT SURE when tongue depressors and Popsicle sticks migrated from doctors' offices and ice cream shops to craft stores, but somewhere along the way they were renamed "craft sticks" and now come in a variety of colors and sizes from mini to jumbo. Although they're great for spreading paste, eating ice cream, and checking sore throats, they also make some fun toys like the three you'll find here.

FACTS ABOUT CRAFT STICKS

- ◆ Wooden craft sticks (tongue depressors and Popsicle sticks) are usually made from birch trees because birch is easy to cut and it's cheap.
- ◆ Jerome Lemelson invented a lighted tongue depressor when he was a kid. He made it for his father, who was a doctor. Lemelson went on to invent technology used to make ATMs, cordless phones, and dolls that cry.
- ◆ Eleven-year-old Frank Epperson invented Popsicles by accident. He left his fruit-flavored soda pop outside on a cold day with a stirring stick in it. He first called his invention an Epsicle. Later, when he was an adult, his children renamed the tasty treat "Popsicle."

One-String Bass

Johnny Cash sang "Daddy played bass," but anyone can play this simple one-string number in your own good-time band.

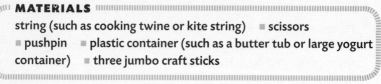

MATERIALS

string (such as cooking twine or kite string) ■ scissors
■ pushpin ■ plastic container (such as a butter tub or large yogurt container) ■ three jumbo craft sticks

Cut a piece of string that's as long as you are tall.

Use the pushpin to make a hole in the center of the bottom of the plastic container.

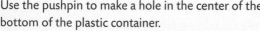

Mark the center of two craft sticks. Gently work a pushpin into the mark to make a hole in the center of each. Don't push too hard or too quickly or you will split the craft stick. (Note: If the craft stick starts to split, don't worry. You can secure the split with a little bit of masking tape.)

Use the pushpin to work the string through the hole in one of the craft sticks. Pull a couple of inches of the string through and tie a several-layer knot so the string won't slip out again.

From the outside of the plastic container, work the long free end of the string through the hole and pull it partway through.

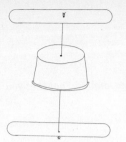

Push an inch of the string through the hole in the other craft stick. Tie a several-layer knot in this end and trim the excess. You will now have a long string with a craft stick at either end and a container between them that you can move.

With the plastic container facing downward, stand with both feet on the craft stick that's below the open mouth of the container, straddling the string. Pull the other craft stick upward so the string is straight up and down in front of you. Wrap the string up and over your shoulder then place the craft stick flat against the front of your shoulder, so that it holds the string snugly under your arm. (Note: If the string is too long, wrap it around the top craft stick to shorten.) Now the string should be taut in front of your body.

With one hand, lift up the plastic container. Use the third craft stick as a pick to pluck the string above the container. Move the container up and down on the string to make different notes. The higher you lift the container, the higher the note.

EXTRA FUN

◆ Try making a bass with a different-sized plastic container and compare the sounds.

◆ Compare how the bass sounds when someone shorter or taller than you plays it.

◆ Make all the musical instruments in this book with your friends and form your own band.

FUN FACT

The washtub bass, or gutbucket, was an early one-string instrument used in American folk music, but this kind of instrument has been found all over the world in some variation.

Opera Singers

These flamboyant singers have big mouths and love to sing loudly . . . not that you would ever sing at the top of your lungs, right?

░▒▓ **MATERIALS** ▓▒░

two jumbo craft sticks (two different-colored ones work nicely for this) ▪ **scissors** ▪ **construction paper** ▪ **glue** ▪ **decorations such as googly eyes, scraps of yarn, tissue paper, felt, sequins, pom-poms, small buttons, and/or glitter (optional)** ▪ **markers** ▪ **chenille stem** ▪ **transparent tape**

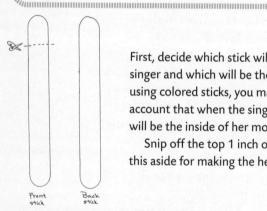

Front
stick

Back
stick

First, decide which stick will be the front of the singer and which will be the back. (Note: If you're using colored sticks, you may want to take into account that when the singer sings, the back stick will be the inside of her mouth.)

Snip off the top 1 inch of the front stick and set this aside for making the head.

Cut a 1 x 2½ inch strip of construction paper. Glue one end to the center of the front stick, perpendicular to the stick. Lay this stick on top of the other one so that their bottoms line up. Wrap the paper around both sticks and secure the loose end with glue. The paper should be tight enough so that the sticks won't fall apart, but with enough play that you can slide the sticks apart with your fingers.

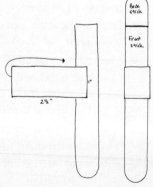

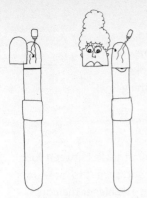

Line up the 1-inch head piece with the exposed top of the back craft stick and glue it in place.

Cut a piece of construction paper in the shape of half of an oval, slightly bigger than the head. Glue this to the front of the head to make the face, lining up the flat edge of the half oval with the flat edge of the head piece. Decorate the face with eyes, a nose, and hair using markers and construction paper, or get more elaborate and use googly eyes, yarn, and/or felt.

Use a marker to draw lips. (Note: The top lip will be on the construction-paper face and the bottom lip will be drawn on the bottom half of the top craft stick.)

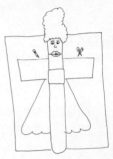

Now make clothes for your singer by laying her on top of a piece of construction paper or felt and drawing the clothing, including arms that stick out to the sides. Be sure to leave 1 inch of the craft sticks peeking out of the bottom of the clothing because this is where you will hold the singer.

Cut out the clothes and decorate. (Remember, opera singers are divas and wear elaborate costumes so you may want to add sequins, glitter, and extra layers of clothing to keep the star of your show happy.)

Next, flip the clothing over and tape a chenille stem across the back so it reaches across both arms. Allow the stem to extend beyond the ends of the arms by ¼ inch (trim the stem if necessary) and secure the stem to the arms with tape. Cut small hands out of paper, and secure one hand to each end of the stem with tape.

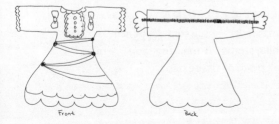

Front   Back

Put a line of glue down the back of the clothing and position it ¼ inch below the bottom lip that you drew. (Remember that 1 inch of the craft sticks should poke out from the bottom of the clothes.) Press the clothing to the craft stick and let dry.

Hold the bottom 1 inch of the craft sticks between your thumb and forefinger. Slide the sticks apart to make your singer open her mouth and sing. The bigger the note, the wider her mouth will have to open. Put her arms in different positions while she performs. Wow, she sure can sing loud, can't she?

EXTRA FUN

◆ Make more singers and stage an opera with your friends.

FUN FACT

Opera singers might be loud, but blue whales and howler monkeys are the loudest living creatures on earth.

Bendy Ballerina and Her Foldable Stage

Here's a great travel toy that folds up and stows easily.

MATERIALS FOR BENDY BALLERINA
two jumbo wooden craft sticks ▪ scissors ▪ pencil ▪ ruler ▪ pushpin ▪ two chenille stems ▪ masking tape ▪ markers ▪ yarn ▪ glue ▪ small piece of tissue paper

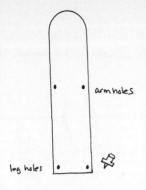

arm holes

leg holes

Use scissors to cut one craft stick in half. You will work with one of these halves to make Bendy Ballerina's body. The rounded end will be the top, and the straight, cut end will be the bottom.

With a pencil, make two dots ¼ inch from the bottom edge and ¼ inch from either side. These will be where you attach the chenille stem legs. Craft sticks split easily, so very carefully poke the pushpin through one dot. Gently twist and turn the pushpin to open the hole. (Note: If the craft stick starts to split, don't worry. You can secure the split with a little bit of masking tape.) Do the same on the other dot.

Make two more dots halfway down the craft stick ¼ inch from either edge, where you will attach the chenille stem arms. As you did with the leg holes, carefully and gently use the pushpin to make holes.

Cut the chenille stems in half. With your fingers, pluck off the top ½ inch of fuzz to expose the wire on one piece. Carefully work the wire of this stem through one of the leg holes. Then wrap the wire end over the bottom of the craft stick and twist it around the chenille-covered part of the stem. Repeat for the other leg and both arms.

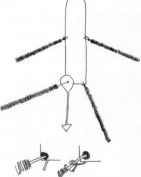

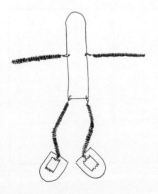

To make the feet, cut a 1-inch section from both ends of the other whole craft stick, so you have two round-edged pieces. Fold ¾ inch of the bottom of one chenille stem leg at a 90-degree angle (like a foot). Lay this segment on top of one of the foot pieces (rounded end pointing forward) and secure with masking tape. Do the same for the other foot. Now your Bendy Ballerina will stand up.

Use markers to draw a face. Glue on bits of yarn for hair. If you want to make a tutu, cut a 3 x 8 inch strip of tissue paper. Tape one end onto the back of the body, crosswise at the waist, then lightly crumple the tissue paper around the stick, securing it with a bit of tape as you go.

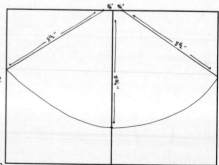

MATERIALS FOR THE FOLDABLE STAGE

two letter-sized manila file folders ▪ scissors ▪ ½-inch-wide masking tape ▪ markers or crayons ▪ pencil ▪ ruler

Trim off any tabs on one file folder so each side measures 8½ x 12 inches. Label this folder A. It will be the back of your stage.

Lay the other folder on your workspace and open it so you see the inside. Make sure the center fold seam runs vertically. At the top of the folder, make a mark ¾ inch to the right and to the left of the seam.

From one of these dots, measure down one side of the folder 8½ inches. Repeat on the other side. From the center of the seam, measure down 8¾ inches. Draw an arc from the left-side 8½-inch mark through the center 8¾-inch mark to the right-side 8½-inch mark.

Cut along this arc so you end up with a piece that looks like this. This is the bottom of the stage.

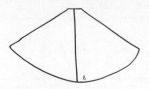

Flip it over so that the inside of the folder is facing down and the arc is near you. Label it B.

Decorate A (the back of the stage) and B (the bottom of the stage), making sure you draw on the inside of folder A and the outside of folder B as these are the sides you'll see when you attach them to one another.

inside of A

OUTSIDE (OR BACK) of B

Stand A on top of B so that their center fold seams meet and are lined up, perpendicular to one another. Then move folder A so there is a ½-inch border of B exposed in the back.

Cut four 8½-inch lengths of ½-inch-wide masking tape. Use them to secure the front and back of folder A to folder B along the line where they meet.

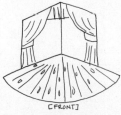

[FRONT]
LINE UP SEAMS

[BACK]
MOVE A FORWARD
½" & Tape A to B

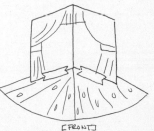

[FRONT]
TAPE A to B

Now set up your stage, cue the music, and see how Bendy Ballerina can dance.

When the performance is over, fold up the stage and slip Bendy inside.

EXTRA FUN

◆ Make a disco dancer or a beat boy and dance floor instead of a ballerina.

FUN FACT

Toe shoes, or pointe shoes, have a small box built around the toe to help ballerinas dance on their tiptoes, called en pointe, for long periods of time.

DRiNK CONTAiNER PROJECTS

DON'T RECYCLE THOSE soda bottles, milk cartons, and juice boxes just yet. First have a look at these fun projects, from boats to bowling alleys.

FACTS ABOUT DRiNK CONTAiNERS

♦ The first containers used to carry drinks were probably hollowed-out gourds or pouches made from animal stomachs.

♦ John Van Wormer, who owned a toy factory in Toledo, Ohio, perfected the first usable paper milk carton in 1915 after he broke a glass milk bottle one day.

♦ Now milk cartons are made from paperboard coated with waterproof plastic.

♦ The spout on today's cartons didn't come around until the 1960s. Before that you had to cut open the container to pour.

♦ Soda used to come in glass bottles until 1970, when Pepsi started using 2-liter plastic bottles.

♦ In 2009, two different inventors made large oceangoing boats out of recycled plastic bottles as a way to promote renewable resources.

Simple Milk Carton Boat

Here are four variations on a theme. Start with the simplest milk carton boat then add on for more elaborate models to follow.

⁞⁞⁞⁞⁞ **MATERIALS** ⁞⁞⁞

½-gallon beverage carton (empty, clean, and dry) ▪ marker
▪ ruler ▪ utility knife ▪ stapler ▪ duct tape

Open the top of the carton all the way. Notice that two of the top panels fold and two are flat. Measure and make a dot in the center of each of the flat top panels. Then draw a line down the center of the carton on these two sides.

Use the utility knife to cut the milk carton in half lengthwise along the lines you drew. Stop when you get to the bottom. *Do not* cut through the center of the bottom. Instead, after you've cut both sides, cut all the way around the bottom so this piece stays intact. The carton half with the bottom attached is

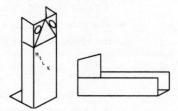

your boat. (Note: If your milk carton has a plastic spout hole at the top end, just cut around it and remove it.)

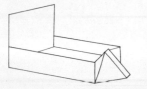

Place the bottom of the boat (which is the long flat side of your carton) on your workspace. Fold the edges of the top panel up so that the carton comes to a point. Staple the edges together to form the boat's bow (that's the front, for us landlubbers). To make your boat seaworthy, reinforce the bow seam with duct tape.

Launch your boat.

Simple Milk Carton Sailboat

Catch the wind with the Tyvek sail on this simple schooner.

MATERIALS

same as for the simple milk carton boat (page 80)   ■ scissors
   ■ 12-inch bamboo skewer   ■ Tyvek envelope   ■ permanent markers

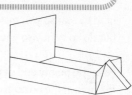

Follow the directions on page 80 for the simple milk carton boat.

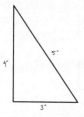

Use the leftover piece of milk carton to make a rudder. Draw a right triangle that measures 3 x 4 x 5 inches. Cut out the triangle and set it aside.

From the inside of the boat, mark the center of the bottom. Make a small hole at this mark by working the pointed tip of the bamboo skewer through the cardboard. (You may need to start the hole with one leg of the scissors, but be very careful so you don't rip the carton.)

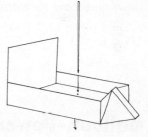

To make the sail, cut the seams of the Tyvek envelope and splay the envelope out to get one large piece. Draw a 6 x 8 inch rectangle. Cut out the rectangle and decorate with permanent markers. (Note: The 8-inch sides will be the top and bottom of the sail; the 6-inch sides will be the sides.)

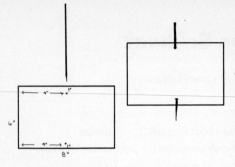

Lay the sail in front of you. Measure 4 inches from a side and 1 inch from the top. Make a mark. Do the same 1 inch from the bottom. Poke the pointy end of the bamboo skewer through the top hole, then push the skewer along until you can poke it back the other way through the bottom hole. (Note: Tyvek is hard to tear so you may need to weaken the fibers with one leg of the scissors, but do so gently so you don't rip the Tyvek.)

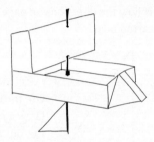

Poke the pointy end of the skewer through the hole in the bottom of the boat so that it extends 3 inches beyond the bottom. Then use duct tape to attach the 3-inch side of the rudder to the bottom 3 inches of the skewer. The 4-inch side of the rudder should be up against the bottom of the boat.

Wind a piece of duct tape around the skewer just above the bottom of the boat to keep the skewer from slipping.

Sail away!

Balloon-Powered Boat

A dual-twin engine of air expulsion sends this boat skimming across the water.

MATERIALS

same as for the simple milk carton boat or sailboat (page 80)
■ hole punch   ■ two balloons

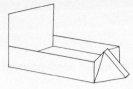

Follow the directions for the simple milk carton boat or sailboat on page 80, then . . .

Use the hole punch (or one leg of a pair of scissors) to make two holes, ½ inch in from each side of the back (or "stern," as seafaring folks call it) and 1½ inches from the top. It may take some persuading to get the hole punch through the heavy bottom of the carton, but you can do it!

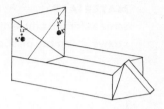

Pull the mouth of a balloon through each hole, from the inside of the boat to the outside, so that the mouthpiece (the curled lip) sticks out of the back of the boat.

Blow up one balloon and pinch it closed while you blow up the other. Pinch the other. Set the boat in the water, let go of the balloons, and watch your boat zip across the bathtub (or "salty drink," if you're a seafarer).

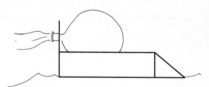

Airboats are flat-bottomed boats with a giant propeller, which looks like a fan, above the water line. The boats move forward as the propeller pushes air out the back. Airboats have no brakes and can't go backward, so don't try to parallel park one.

FUN FACT

Propeller Boat

Step up your marina with this milk carton boat and its rubber band–powered propeller.

||||||| **MATERIALS** ||||||||||||||||||||||||||||||||||||||||||||||||||||||||||

same as for the simple milk carton boat (page 80) ▪ two drinking
straws ▪ empty plastic spool ▪ paper clip ▪ rubber band

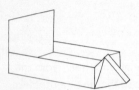

Follow the directions for the simple milk carton boat on page 80, then . . .

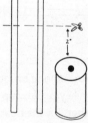

Trim both straws so they are 2 inches longer than the spool, then set them aside for later.

Hold the spool against the center of the back/stern of the boat close to the bottom. Trace the circle with a permanent marker.

Use a ruler to draw four straight lines, crossing in the center of the circle (so it looks like an asterisk). Cut along these lines with a utility knife. (Hint: Work slowly and carefully by cutting from the outer edge of the circle toward the center so that you don't rip the carton.)

From the outside of the boat, gently push the spool through the hole until the pieces you cut lie flat against the sides of the spool. Secure these with a long strip of duct tape around the spool. Take a look for any unseaworthy areas of your boat and reinforce these with more duct tape.

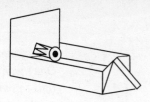

Slip the paper clip over one end of the rubber band, then push the paper clip through one

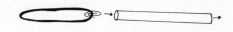

straw and pull it out the other side, leaving part of the rubber band hanging out of the opposite end of the straw.

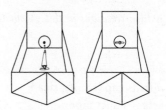

From the inside of the boat, push the straw, rubber band end first, through the center hole in the spool. Secure the paper clip flat against the end of the spool with duct tape.

Put the other straw through the loop of the rubber band on the outside of the boat. This straw is your propeller.

Twist the propeller many, many times until the rubber band is taut inside the spool straw. You have to wind the rubber band really tight to make this work. Sometimes, though, the rubber band will be uncooperative at first (rubber bands are like that). A good snap of the propeller usually gets things going. Put your boat in the water and watch it put-put along as the propeller spins.

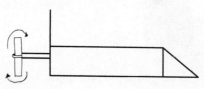

EXTRA FUN

◆ Become a shipping magnate with your own fleet of simple boats, balloon-powered boats, and propeller boats.

◆ Take your clothespin people (page 60) for a ride in your boats.

Lots of people invented propellers for boats in the 1800s. One inventor took his idea from the way fish move their tails to swim through the water. Another inventor was inspired by a windmill.

Rice Hunt

Shake a plastic bottle full of rice to uncover hidden treasures in this excellent travel toy.

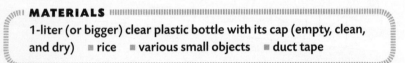

MATERIALS

1-liter (or bigger) clear plastic bottle with its cap (empty, clean, and dry) ▪ rice ▪ various small objects ▪ duct tape

Remove the label from the bottle then fill it two-thirds of the way with rice.

Scrounge around your house for small objects that can easily fit through the opening of the soda bottle (e.g., tiny cars, dolls, marbles, dice, bolts, magnets, pennies, and rubber balls). Make a list of all the objects as you drop them into the bottle.

Check List
Dice
Penny
Marble
Ball
Game piece

Put the cap on the bottle and reinforce with duct tape.

Shake the bottle furiously until the objects are mixed into the rice.

Take turns shaking, spinning, and turning the bottle every which way to see what hidden treasures you can spot.

EXTRA FUN

◆ Have a contest to see who can find the most objects in one minute.

◆ Make a checklist of items inside the bottle. For readers, write the words. For pre-readers, draw pictures.

◆ Every so often, dump the contents out and change the treasures.

Soda Bottle and Rolling Pin Bowling Alley

This is a simple and fun way to keep things rolling along on a rainy day.

MATERIALS

six 1-liter plastic bottles (empty, clean, and dry) ▪ masking tape ▪ rolling pin

Set the bottles up in a triangle arrangement at the end of a room with a long, smooth floor.

Use masking tape to make a starting line 3 feet away from the front bottle (one point of the triangle should face you) and place the rolling pin on the line.

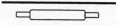

Take turns pushing the rolling pin toward the soda bottles. Score how many bottles each player knocks over.

EXTRA FUN

◆ Use ten bottles.

◆ Fill the bottles with rice or dried beans or jingle bells so they make fun noises when knocked over.

◆ Move the starting line farther away.

FUN FACT

Bowling is usually played with ten pins and a large, heavy ball that has three to five finger holes. The balls weigh between 6 and 16 pounds.

Teeny Tiny Air Rocket

Based on a stomp rocket, this small tabletop version is out of this world.

MATERIALS

flexible drinking straw* ■ scissors ■ juice box (empty, clean, and dry) ■ paper ■ ruler ■ pencil ■ transparent tape

* Note: You need a regular-sized flexible drinking straw (not the tiny one that comes with a juice box, which is too small).

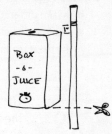

First, trim the bottom of the straw so that the flexible tip will stick out 1 inch beyond the top of the box when you push it inside.

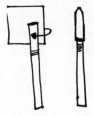

Make a rocket by cutting out a 2 x 2 inch square of paper. Roll the square around the flexible end of the straw and secure the seam with tape. Pinch the top of the paper closed and secure that with tape as well.

Slip the nonflexible end of the straw through the hole in the top of the box until it touches the inside bottom of the box and the flexible end of the straw sticks out the top. Secure the straw to the top of the box with tape.

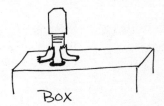

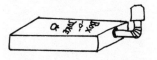

Lay the box on its side (so that the wide flat side is down). Bend the straw so that the tip, with the rocket on the end, faces the ceiling.

Whack the juice box and watch your rocket fly!

When you're done, blow into the straw to reinflate the juice box, put another rocket on the end, and go again.

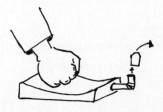

EXTRA FUN

◆ Make different shapes and sizes of rockets with other drink boxes.

◆ Have a rocket contest with a friend: Whose rocket can go highest or farthest, or land in a cup the most times?

The first drink boxes, called Tetra Briks, were invented in the 1960s, but juice boxes didn't come around until the 1980s.

FABRIC PROJECTS

DON'T BE PUT off by this section if you're not comfortable with a needle and thread. Most of these are no-sew projects using fabric you'll find around the house or can pick up at a craft store.

FACTS ABOUT FABRIC

◆ Human beings have been sewing and weaving by hand since prehistoric times.

◆ Felt, which was originally made by pressing together wool fibers, is probably the oldest kind of fabric in the world.

◆ The first sewing needles were made from animal bones.

◆ Historically, fabric has been made from plant and animal sources (such as cotton and wool), but some modern fabrics, such as Polarfleece, are made from recycled plastic bottles.

◆ George de Mestral invented Velcro (hook-and-loop fasteners) after studying how burrs clung to his hunting clothes.

Jingle Jumpers

Old socks and a few bells make fantastic wrist and ankle instruments.

MATERIALS

old sock ■ scissors ■ four safety pins ■ four jingle bells

Cut the cuff off the sock. Discard the foot part.

Fold the cut edge up ¼ inch, then pull the top of the sock down to meet the fold you just made. Now the cuff is folded in half with the cut edge folded inside.

Turn the cuff so the two edges (top of the sock and the folded cut edge) face up. From the inside of the cuff, stick a safety pin through both edges as close to the top as you can get.

Slip a jingle bell over the pointy arm of the pin on the outside of the cuff. Stick the pin back through the cuff and clip it on the inside. Pin the other three bells evenly around the cuff.

Put your jingle jumper around your ankle or wrist and jump around to make music.

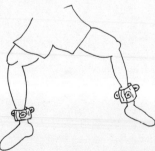

EXTRA FUN

◆ Make all the musical instruments in this book with your friends and form your own band.

FUN FACT

Sleigh bells (which are large jingle bells) were the first instruments played in space. Astronauts Wally Schirra and Tom Stafford pretended to see Santa Claus from their Gemini 6 spacecraft, then played "Jingle Bells" on a harmonica and sleigh bells.

Sock Baby

This is one of the simplest no-sew baby dolls around.

MATERIALS
colorful children's sock ▪ polyfill or other stuffing ▪ embroidery floss or other string ▪ ribbon ▪ permanent marker

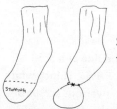

Stuff the toe of a sock (about one-quarter of the foot) with polyfill. Tie it off with embroidery floss.

Stuff the rest of the foot with polyfill and tie this off with embroidery floss also. Now you have a head (the toe) and a body (the rest of the foot). The rest of the sock (the part that would go over the ankle) is empty.

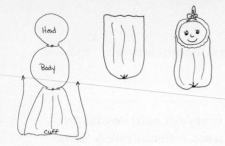

Hold the sock so the head faces up. Fold the cuff of the sock up over the body and head. Roll down the front so the face peeks out. Gather a bit of the sock cuff at the top (on top of the head) and tie it off with a ribbon.

Use a permanent marker to draw eyes, nose, and a mouth on the face.

EXTRA FUN

◆ Take your baby for a ride in the shoe box baby carriage on page 164.

FUN FACT

Before automatic sock-knitting machines were introduced in the mid-1800s, people knit socks at home by hand. People have been making stuffed animals and puppets out of their socks for a very long time.

Dress-Up Doll Frame

This is a good travel toy for any budding fashion designer.

MATERIALS

large piece of corrugated cardboard (such as the side of a box)
■ pencil ■ ruler ■ scissors ■ utility knife ■ 8½ x 11 inch white drawing paper ■ masking tape ■ markers ■ various scraps of fabric (such as from old clothes, handkerchiefs, sheets, or towels)

Cut two 10 x 12 inch rectangles out of the cardboard. Set one aside. On the other one, draw an 8 x 10 inch rectangle in the center and cut it out using the utility knife so it looks like a picture frame with a 2-inch border.

 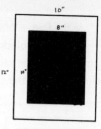

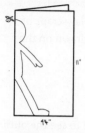

Fold the paper in half lengthwise and draw the shape of half a person's body (lengthwise) in the center of the paper, next to the fold (as shown) or trace the template on page 211. With the paper still folded, cut out the body.

Unfold the paper. You now have a cutout person and the shape of a person cut out in the center of the paper. Set aside the cutout person and keep the paper with the shape cut out for this project.

Keep

Set aside

Choose one side of the frame to be the front, and lay it front side down on your work surface. Tape the paper along all four of its edges to the frame so that the person is now in the center of the frame.

Turn the frame around on your workspace if necessary (with the taped side still up) so the head is facing you. Place your set-aside piece of cardboard below it so the short sides meet. Use one long piece of masking tape to join the frame and other piece of cardboard together along the short side.

Close the frame. Draw hair around the head on the paper.
Then use a black marker to trace the shape of the person onto the cardboard underneath. Draw a face on the person on the cardboard underneath.

To play with the frame, open it and lay scraps of fabric over the body of the person drawn on the cardboard.

Close the frame to see the outfit you made! Change the fabric to make new outfits.

EXTRA FUN

- ◆ Make smaller or larger frames and people.
- ◆ To make your person wear a dress or skirt, cut out a skirt shape from the waist to the knees on the paper so it looks like this:
- ◆ Draw different characters (such as a ballerina, race car driver, or clown).
- ◆ Draw your pets (dogs, cats, fish, or what-have-you) to see how they'd look in cool duds.

FUN FACT

A pattern cutter is a person who turns a fashion designer's sketch of clothing into a working pattern that can be used to make the clothes.

No-Sew Felt Coin Purse

Save those nickels, dimes, and small treasures to stow in this quick and easy coin purse.

MATERIALS
ruler ▪ white chalk ▪ 12 x 12 inch piece of brightly colored felt ▪ scissors ▪ self-adhesive hook-and-loop fasteners ▪ fabric glue

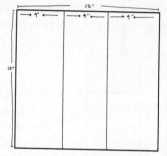

Using a ruler and white chalk, draw two straight lines from the top to the bottom of the felt square 4 inches from each side, so that you end up with three equal vertical sections (each 4 inches wide).

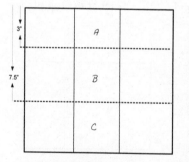

Measure and mark two dotted chalk lines, one 3 inches from the top and the other 7½ inches from the top. These dotted lines give you three sections (A over B over C). When complete, section A (3 inches) will be the flap of the coin purse, section B (4½ inches) will be the back, and section C (4½ inches) will be the front.

Next, fold the felt in half lengthwise so that the chalk lines face out. Only one of the vertical lines, and half of each dotted line, will show. Make sure the edges of the felt are lined up neatly.

With the chalk, draw a horizontal line from the outside (not the folded) edge of the felt to the vertical line, ¼ inch from the bottom edge. Draw another line ¼ inch above that, and repeat until you reach the dotted line that marks the top of section B. Then use the scissors to cut along these lines from the outside edge to the vertical chalk line so that you seem to be making fringe along the edge of the felt. (Note: Cut through the front and back piece of felt at the same time. If the felt is slipping, safety pin the top and bottom to hold it in place.)

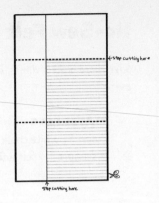

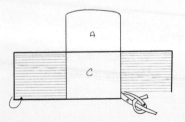

With the fabric still folded, cut through both layers of felt along the vertical line in section A only, so that this piece of section A, from the edge to the vertical line, comes off. Round off the corner at the top of the vertical line.

Open the felt and lay it flat. It should look like this.

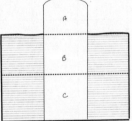

Now, fold section C over section B. Tie knots with the ¼-inch strips you cut on the edges. You will tie one strip from section C with the corresponding strip from section B (which is behind C now). Do this on both sides of the purse.

Trim the excess off the knots.

Trim a 1-inch square of hook-and-loop fastener.
Center a dot of fabric glue on the inside of the top flap
(section A), near the top, and attach the square. (If you
can find self-adhesive squares, all the better!) Fold the
flap down and put a dot of fabric glue where the other
half of the hook-and-loop fastener should go.

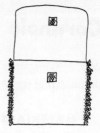

Close the flap and add a decoration to the outside
front of the flap if you want, then store your
treasures in your purse.

EXTRA FUN

◆ Use scraps of different-colored felt and the fabric glue to decorate the
coin purse.
◆ Try making different sizes.

*Originally, pockets were small bags that people tied
around their waists and tucked inside their clothing to
keep money and other important things. Then somebody
got the bright idea of sewing pockets into the clothing
and cutting a slit so you could reach your hand inside.*

Cornhole

Where I'm originally from in Indiana, folks call this game cornhole. Of course, in the interest of regional diversity, you could always call it a beanbag toss instead.

MATERIALS FOR THE BEANBAGS

12 x 12 inch square of felt ▪ ruler ▪ white pencil or chalk ▪ pinking shears or regular scissors ▪ iron-on decal and iron (optional) ▪ embroidery floss or strong thread ▪ needle ▪ popcorn kernels or dried beans

Use pinking shears to cut two 4 x 4 inch squares of felt. Iron the decal onto the center of one square if you want, then place the squares on top of one another so that the decal faces up.

Use a strand of embroidery floss to sew the felt layers together, making a seam around three sides, ½ inch from the edges. Sew halfway up the fourth side, leaving a long length of floss to complete the last edge later.

Fill the bag with popcorn kernels or dried beans.

Sew up the rest of the final seam, knot the floss, and cut.

MATERIALS FOR THE TARGET BOX

medium-sized cardboard box ▪ utility knife ▪ pencil ▪ ruler
or yardstick ▪ poster paint, markers, and/or stickers (optional)

Cut off the top flaps of your box. Then turn the box on its side so one of the long sides faces up and the opening faces toward you. On the side facing up, draw a line from the top left corner to the bottom right corner, bisecting the long side diagonally.

Flip the box over so the opposite side faces up and the opening still faces you. This time, draw a line from the top right corner to the bottom left corner, again bisecting the long side diagonally.

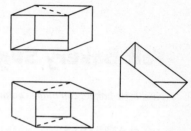

Use the utility knife to cut along the line on one side, then across the bottom of the narrow end, then up the line on the opposite side.

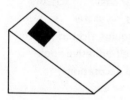

Set the box on your workspace with the open side down and the flat side facing up so it looks like a ramp. Draw a 6 x 6 inch square centered 3 inches from the top. Use a utility knife to cut out the square.

Decorate the target box with construction paper, paint, markers, and/or stickers if you like.

To Play

Place the target a few feet away and try to toss the corn bag into the hole.

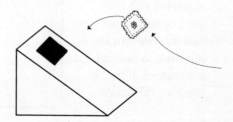

◆ Cornhole is played with two targets and eight corn bags (four for each player). Set the targets up directly across from one another as far apart as makes sense for the players. Take turns trying to toss your corn bags into the targets. Corn bags that land in the hole are worth three points. Corn bags that land on the target without touching the ground are worth one point.

Felt Bakery Sugar Cookie Factory

Now little bakers can make cookies even when the kitchen's closed.

MATERIALS

light brown felt squares ▪ lids from various plastic containers (such as yogurt or margarine tubs) ▪ white pencil or chalk ▪ scissors ▪ fabric glue ▪ additional felt in various colors ▪ glitter ▪ additional decorations such as jewels, beads, sequins, rickrack, fabric flowers, and/or pretty buttons (optional) ▪ self-adhesive hook-and-loop fastener dots (optional, for additional decorations)

Trace the lids onto the brown felt with the white pencil or chalk then cut them out and glue them to the tops and bottoms of the lids. These are the cookies.

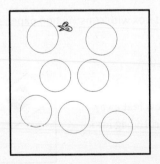

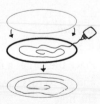

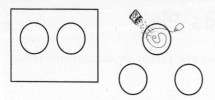

While the cookies are drying, cut out slightly smaller circles in different-colored felt to make frosting. Make glue designs on some of the frosting circles and cover with glitter to make sprinkles.

While the glue is drying, cut out decorations from the other pieces of felt, such as flowers, stars, circles, and swirls. These will stick to the tops of the cookies (because felt sticks to felt).

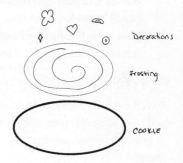

If you want to make fancier cookies, put the hook side of self-adhesive hook-and-loop fastener dots on the backs of pretty buttons, fabric roses, rickrack, jewels, etc. These will stick directly to the felt cookies.

Decorate your cookies!

EXTRA FUN

◆ Put your cookies on a cookie sheet and "bake" them inside a cardboard box oven.
◆ Display your cookies on pretty platters.
◆ Make a bakery to sell your cookies, pies (page 104), and cakes (page 106) to all the hungry people.

FUN FACT

Food historians think cookies were probably first made as test cakes to make sure the oven temperature was correct.

Felt Bakery Easy-as-Pie

This is the easiest no-bake pie you'll ever find. Best of all, you can make endless varieties without a messy kitchen.

MATERIALS

two 12 x 12 inch light brown felt squares ▪ 8-inch plate ▪ white pencil or chalk ▪ scissors ▪ 6-inch aluminum foil pie pan ▪ fabric glue ▪ self-adhesive hook-and-loop fastener dots ▪ scraps of felt in various colors ▪ small pom-poms and/or beads

Turn the 8-inch plate upside down and trace around it onto one piece of brown felt, then cut out the circle.

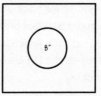 

Cover the inside bottom of the pie pan with fabric glue. Center the 8-inch felt circle over the pan then push down evenly so the felt sticks to the glue on the bottom. (Note: You will have extra felt sticking up around the inside edge of the pie pan.)

Working in small sections, cover the inside edge of the pan with some glue and press the loose felt down. Work your way around the pan until all the fabric is stuck to the pie pan. (Remember, pies aren't perfect, so some wrinkles in the fabric are fine.) Set aside to dry. Then put a line of glue around the rim of the pie pan and press the edge of the fabric down.

For the top crust, turn the 6-inch pie pan upside down and trace around the outside of the other piece of brown felt. (If you want a fancy pie crust, sketch a scalloped edge around the outside of the circle and then cut it out. For a plain crust, just cut around the circle.)

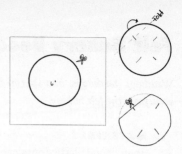

Use the chalk or white pencil to mark four steam slits in the center of the top crust, then fold the felt over at each slit and snip.

To attach the top crust to the bottom, put eight pieces of self-adhesive hook-and-loop fasteners around the top edge of the bottom crust and corresponding pieces around the bottom edge of the top crust.

Use the other colors of felt to cut out different pie fillings (apples, strawberries, cherries). You can also use pom-poms or beads to make berries.

Fill the pie with fruit, cover with the top crust, and pop it in your "oven."

EXTRA FUN

◆ Make a bakery to sell your pies, cookies (page 102), and cakes (page 106) to all the hungry people.

FUN FACT

The first pies were called coffins. They had meat inside the crust. Later, animated pies were popular banquet entertainment. These were giant pies with live animals or even people inside who popped out, like in the nursery rhyme "Sing a Song of Sixpence," which says, "When the pie was opened, the birds began to sing."

Felt Bakery Decorate-a-Cake Kit

Weddings, birthdays, and special occasions are always better with a beautiful cake from the felt bakery.

MATERIALS

deep, round plastic container with a lid* ▪ two 12 x 12 inch squares of white felt** ▪ colored pencil or chalk ▪ scissors ▪ fabric glue ▪ additional decorations such as jewels, rickrack, fabric flowers, pretty buttons (optional) ▪ white self-adhesive hook-and-loop fastener dots (optional, for additional decorations)

* Note: I used a 7-cup disposable container that is 4½ inches tall and 7 inches across the top opening, but you could use any size as long as it looks sort of like a cake when you flip it upside down. If you use a different size container, adjust the measurements accordingly.

** Note: If you can find felt by the yard, buy ⅓ yard or whatever amount you need to cover a smaller or larger container.

Remove the lid from the container and set aside. Turn the bowl upside down.

Cut one square of white felt in half so you have two 6 x 12 inch pieces. Run a line of fabric glue along the long edge of one piece of white felt. Wrap the felt around the bowl so the line of glue adheres just above the lip of the bowl (which is now the bottom of your cake). Then run a line of glue around the outside edge at the top of the cake (which is the outside bottom of the bowl, turned upside down) and press the felt against the bowl to glue it in place.

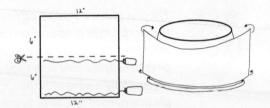

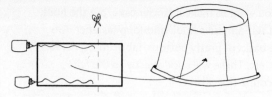

Trim the other piece of fabric long enough to cover the rest of the side of the bowl, with a little bit extra. Glue this piece of felt to the bowl in the same way. (Note: The second piece of felt will overlap the first.) Let dry.

Run a line of glue around the top edge of the cake (i.e., the bottom of the bowl). Start at the corner of one piece of felt. Press the felt edge over onto the top of the cake so that a bit of it sticks to the glue. Now you will have a small fold in the fabric between where it attaches and the rest of the fabric that sticks up. Use scissors to snip this fold, then overlap the felt, and press the next bit into the glue. Every time you press a bit down, you'll have a small fold. Continue folding and snipping in this way around the cake until all of the felt is attached to the bowl. Then, secure any small loose flaps of felt with a bit more glue.

Turn the cake upside down (so the open side faces up and the bottom of the bowl is facing down). Set it in the center of the remaining square of white felt. Draw a circle around the bowl, then cut it out. Flip the cake over again so the opening faces down. Cover the top of the cake (which is the bottom of the bowl) with glue and press the circle of felt on it. Set aside to dry.

While the glue is drying, cut out decorations from the other pieces of felt, such as flowers, stars, circles, and/or swirls. These will stick to the sides of the cake (because felt sticks to felt).

If you want to make a fancier cake, put the hook side of self-adhesive hook-and-loop fastener dots on the backs of pretty buttons, fabric roses, rickrack, jewels, etc. These will stick directly to the felt.

Decorate the cake!

When you're done, place all the decorations inside the bowl and put the lid on.

EXTRA FUN

◆ Make a bakery to sell your cakes, cookies (page 102), and pies (page 104) to all the hungry people.

FUN FACT

The tradition of putting candles on a birthday cake may have come from the ancient Greeks, who took small cakes (shaped like the moon and topped with candles) to the temple of Artemis.

Pizzeria

Pizza fiends will love this pretend pizzeria, complete with a rolling cutter.

MATERIALS FOR THE FELT BOARD PIZZA*

scraps of felt in various colors (green, red, yellow, brown) ■ 6-inch plate or lid ■ corrugated cardboard or cardboard cake round** ■ marker ■ utility knife ■ 8-inch plate or lid ■ ½ yard of light brown felt ■ scissors ■ fabric glue ■ masking tape

* Note: These are the instructions for making a 6-inch round pizza, but you could make whatever size and shape you want. Adjust the measurements accordingly.

** Note: Some wedding supply craft stores sell premade cardboard cake rounds. You could also use the round piece of cardboard from an actual pizza box.

Trace the 6-inch plate on the cardboard. Use a utility knife or scissors to cut out the cardboard circle. Note: Circles can be difficult to cut out of heavy cardboard, so first trim the cardboard in a

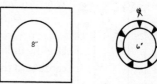

square as close to the edges of the circle as you can. Then work slowly in curved sections rather than trying to make one clean cut all the way around.

Trace the 8-inch plate on the light brown felt then cut out the felt circle.
   Center the cardboard circle on top of the felt circle so there is a 2-inch border around the edge. Use the marker to draw a V-shaped notch every 2 inches around the border. Snip out the notches to create a series of tabs around the outside.

Put a dot of fabric glue on each felt tab, then fold it over the cardboard and press down. Reinforce with masking tape. (Hint: Glue the first tab down, then glue the one opposite to it. Continue in this way so the fabric is always

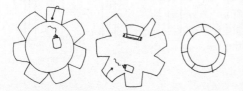

pulled taut.) Do this for all the tabs, making sure you pull the felt tight as you go. You may want to put a heavy book on top as this dries. When it's done, this is the pizza dough!

Now make the toppings from the scraps:

- ◆ 4-inch red circle for sauce
- ◆ tan or brown for mushrooms
- ◆ red half circles for pepperoni
- ◆ strips of yellow or white for cheese
- ◆ green moons for green peppers
- ◆ gray fish for anchovies

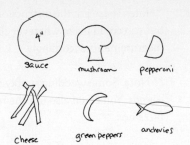

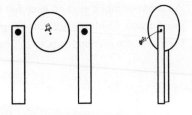

MATERIALS FOR THE PIZZA CUTTER

leftover cardboard from the pizza board ▪ ruler ▪ pencil
▪ utility knife ▪ hole punch ▪ plastic lid from a small
container ▪ pushpin ▪ small prong paper fastener ▪ red
masking tape (or masking tape and a red marker)

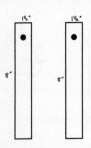

Use the utility knife to cut two 1½ x 8 inch strips of cardboard then punch a hole near the end of one piece. Lay it on top of the other and mark the hole, then punch out the hole in the second piece.

Use a pushpin to poke a hole in the center of the plastic lid.

Put the lid between the two strips of cardboard so that the holes all line up. Poke the prong paper fastener through and bend the legs outward to hold the lid in place between the cardboard strips.

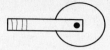

Tape the other ends of the cardboard together with red masking tape to form the handle.

EXTRA FUN

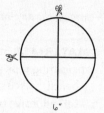

- ◆ If you want to be able to cut the pizza, cut the 6-inch cardboard circle into four equal pieces.
  - ■ To cover the cardboard pieces with felt, you'll need to trace a 10-inch plate on the felt, then cut the circle into four equal pie-shaped pieces.
  - ■ Center a triangular piece of cardboard over each piece of felt. Snip the corners off and notch the top curve as shown. Then glue the edges, fold over, and tape.

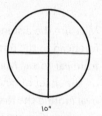

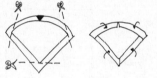

- ■ Cut the 4-inch red sauce circle into four equal pie-shaped pieces. Put the pizza pieces together to form a circle. Add toppings, "bake" it, and cut to serve.

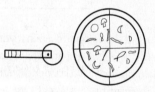

Americans love pizza. We eat about 350 slices per second in the United States.

FUN FACT

Master of Disguises

Slip through the day incognito in one of these felt masks.

MATERIALS

measuring tape (or a length of string and a ruler) ▪ newspaper ▪ pencil ▪ scissors ▪ 12 x 12 inch felt squares in various colors ▪ self-adhesive hook-and-loop fastener tape ▪ thin, round elastic cord or large rubber band ▪ marker ▪ straight pin

Make a Template of Your Face

Measure the distance from the top of your forehead to the bottom of your chin and from ear to ear. Mark these measurements on the sheet of newspaper, then draw a large oval around the marks roughly the shape of your face. Cut out the template.

Hold the template against your face, making sure it's the right size and shape to cover your face completely. With a pencil, lightly sketch around the area of your eyes or ask a friend to help. Next, lightly sketch a line where your lips meet.

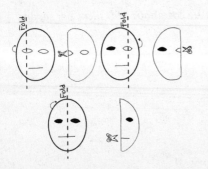

With the template away from your face, find the center of one eye. Fold the newspaper lengthwise at this point and trim around the eye. Do the same for the other eye.

Find the center point of the lip line. Fold the newspaper lengthwise at this point and cut along the line.

Unfold and press the template against your face to make sure the holes match up to your eyes and lips.

Make the Base of Your Mask

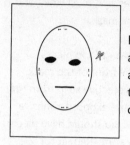

Pin the newspaper template to a felt square. Trim around the face then use the folding technique from above to trim out the eyes and the lip line. Reuse the newspaper template to make other felt faces in different colors.

Cut out pieces of the self-adhesive hook-and-loop fastener tape. Remove the strip covering one side of the adhesive. Press this side on each felt mask as follows: (1) across the forehead (to hold hair or hats), (2) above the eyes (to hold eyebrows), (3) in the center of the face and between the eyes (to hold noses), (4) above and below the mouth (to hold mustaches and lips), and (5) on the chin (to hold beards). Keep the corresponding piece of the fasteners (with the protective strip over the adhesive) attached for now. Later you'll attach them to the facial features you will make below.

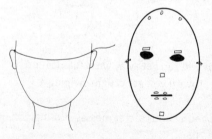

Hold the elastic at the back of one ear, pull it around behind your head to the back of the other ear, and pinch. Snip the elastic where you're pinching.

Hold a felt mask up to your face and make a dot on each side of the mask, just above your ears. Remove the mask from your face and poke a small hole at each mark, then slip the ends of the elastic through the holes, from the back to the front, and tie small knots.

Make the Facial Features

On the other pieces of felt, sketch and cut out a variety of hairstyles, hats, eyebrows, noses, lips, mustaches, and beards to fit the mask.

Keep the hook-and-loop pieces attached on the front of the mask. Remove the protective strip from the adhesive backing, press the facial feature down onto the exposed adhesive to attach, then gently remove the facial feature. Now you should have pieces of hook-and-loop fastener on the mask and on the feature. Repeat for additional features.

Become a Master of Disguises

Attach different features to the hook-and-loop fasteners, then slip the mask over your face so that the elastic runs behind your head and rests on top of your ears.

EXTRA FUN

- ◆ Try lots of disguises and see what you can get away with. Blame it on the weirdo with bushy black eyebrows if you get caught swiping a cookie from the cupboard.
- ◆ While wearing your mask, write anonymous secret messages using one of the invisible inks on page 205.

No-Sew T-Shirt Doll

This is based on an old-fashioned "Nettie" doll that women made from their fabric scraps. Unless you're Ma Ingalls or doing some serious homesteading these days, you probably won't have a scrap bag full of colorful fabric. But you probably do have old T-shirts, which work beautifully for this project.

> **MATERIALS**
>
> old T-shirt (one men's large or multiple shirts to get the measured fabric below) ■ measuring tape or ruler ■ scissors

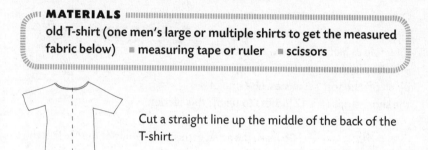

Cut a straight line up the middle of the back of the T-shirt.

Spread the T-shirt on the floor and cut out the largest section of fabric that you can.

You want to end up with forty-two 1 x 18 inch strips plus another twenty-seven 1 x 12 inch strips. To do this, first trim your fabric into a rectangle that is roughly 18 x 42 inches. (The most important part of this is the 18-inch width. If you can't get 42 inches across, cut another section of fabric from the same or a different shirt that is also 18 inches wide.) Along the 42-inch side, make a small snip every 1 inch. Trim another piece of the shirt to 12 x 27 inches (or use multiple shirts). Along the 27-inch edge, make a snip every 1 inch.

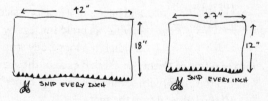

42"
18"
SNIP EVERY INCH

27"
12"
SNIP EVERY INCH

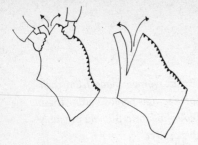

Once you make the snips, you can rip the fabric easily into strips. Starting at one edge, hold the fabric on either side of the first snip, then pull. You'll end up with a 1-inch strip that will curl around the edges. This is fine. Make forty-two of the 18-inch strips and twenty-seven of the 12-inch strips.

Gather the 1 x 18 inch strips into one long bunch. Twist once in the middle, then fold in half so you now have two 9-inch sections. To make the head, pinch off the top 1½ inches. Use one of the short strips (1 x 12 inches) to tie off this section.

To make the arms, gather twenty-one of the 1 x 12 inch strips into one long bunch. (Leave the extra five strips aside for now.) Insert these arm strips through the center of the body strips so they're the same length on either side. Then pinch the body strips together just below the arms (about 1½ inches from where you tied off the head). Tie this off with one of the extra short strips.

Divide one arm into three equal sections (seven strips each) and braid. Tie off the end with one of the extra short strips. Do the same for the other arm. Trim the hands.

At this point, you can be done and have a doll in a long skirt, or you can braid the legs by dividing the long body strips into two sets of twenty-one. Braid each of those as you did the arms (with seven strips in each bunch). Tie off the legs and trim the feet.

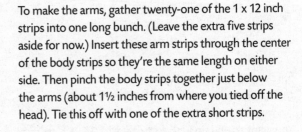

- Make a sundress, apron, or kerchief for your doll out of the leftover T-shirt scraps.
- Take your doll for a ride in the shoe box baby carriage on page 164.

> **FUN FACT**
>
> *T-shirts were originally underwear for men or work shirts for soldiers until Marlon Brando's character Stanley Kowalski wore a plain white T in the 1951 movie* **A Streetcar Named Desire** *and started a fad that has yet to die.*

Secret Cave

A variation on the blanket fort, where spies, secret agents, ninjas, and outlaws like to hide.

MATERIALS

pillows ▪ table ▪ old queen- or king-sized white sheet ▪ pencil ▪ masking tape ▪ black permanent or fabric marker ▪ additional permanent or fabric markers in various colors ▪ scissors

Pile pillows up on top of the table to make a little pyramid shape.

Throw the sheet over the pillows and table and adjust the sides so the front edge touches the ground. With the pencil, sketch the opening of the cave, making it big enough to crawl through.

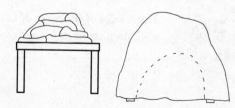

Remove the sheet from the table and find a big empty workspace to spread out the sheet. (To prevent damage to the work surface from the marker bleeding through the sheet, lay down newspaper and secure to the workspace with a bit of masking tape.) Lay the sheet out flat. Tape one end of the sheet to the workspace (but not to the newspaper). Pull the other end taut and tape it down. Tape down the other two sides so that the fabric is smooth and flat.

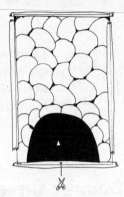

Use the permanent black marker to color in the opening of the cave. Then draw large rocks all around the rest of the cave. With the other markers, embellish the cave with weeds, grass, dirt, etc.

Untape the bottom of the sheet and cut a slit up the center of the opening then untape the rest of the sheet.

Put the sheet back over the pillows and table, arranging it so the opening is in the front again.

EXTRA FUN

- ◆ Be sure to store a flashlight, snacks, and water in the cave.
- ◆ Make things more cozy with blankets and extra pillows inside the cave.

FUN FACT *The insides of the caves of Lascaux, France, are covered with prehistoric paintings showing hunting scenes.*

Castle Curtain

Invite your loyal subjects to enter the royal chamber through the castle door.

MATERIALS

old twin-sized white sheet ▪ scissors ▪ 3-inch-wide masking tape ▪ ruler or yardstick ▪ pencil ▪ black permanent marker ▪ permanent markers of various colors (optional) ▪ spring rod (for hanging curtains) that will fit your doorway ▪ safety pins

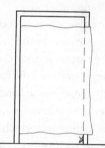

First, find an open doorway where you'd like to hang your castle curtain when it's finished. Hold the sheet up to make sure it's the right size to cover the door opening. You want it to spread out and take up the entire doorway. If it's too wide, snip the edge where it meets the doorjamb. Cut this strip off the sheet and fold the rough edge under, then secure with tape.

Find a big empty workspace. (To prevent damage to your work surface from the marker bleeding through the sheet, lay down newspaper and secure to the workspace with a bit of masking tape.) Lay the sheet out flat. Tape one end of the sheet to the workspace (but not to the newspaper). Pull the other end taut and tape it down. Tape down the other two sides so that the fabric is smooth and flat.

With a pencil, sketch the outside of your castle first, leaving the top 18 inches of the sheet blank. For example, make two tall turrets with parapets in between.

Add a rounded door in the center that is slightly taller than the castle occupants and windows on either side. Once you're happy with your design, use the permanent black marker to go over it with bold lines. If you want to add more color, use additional markers. (If you're really ambitious, use fabric paint.)

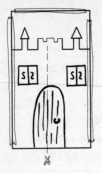

Untape the bottom of the sheet, then cut a slit up the center, stopping 24 inches from the top. Untape the rest of the sheet.

Adjust the spring rod so it's the correct size to fit in your doorway. Flip the sheet over so the back faces up. Place the spring rod 6 inches from the top of the fabric. Fold the top of the fabric over the rod.

Use safety pins to secure the fabric just below the rod. (Make sure the safety pins are on the back side of the curtain so they don't mar the appearance of the castle. Of course, if you're handy with a needle and thread, you could make a quick whipstitch seam to hold the rod inside the fabric.)

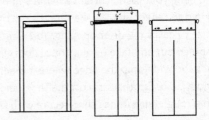

Hang the curtain in the doorway.

EXTRA FUN

◆ Add the castle with a drawbridge (page 42) to your kingdom.

FUN FACT

Windsor Castle, in England, is the largest inhabited castle in the world. It has approximately one thousand rooms.

POSTER BOARD AND FOAM BOARD PROJECTS

VERSATILE, LIGHTWEIGHT, AND easy to find, poster board and its pumped-up cousin, foam board, are excellent resources for home toy makers. Poster board is a large, heavy piece of paper board made especially for decorating with crayons, markers, and acrylic paint. Foam board (also called foam core) is a layer of foam that's been laminated on both sides so it's easy to cut and decorate, but it's sturdier than poster board. Here are a few ideas to get you started, though you'll soon see that the possibilities are endless.

FACTS ABOUT POSTER BOARD AND FOAM BOARD

◆ When most people think of poster boards, they think of school science fairs because students display the results of their science projects on poster boards. Science fairs started in the 1940s as an outgrowth of science clubs and competitions held by a national nonprofit group called Science Service.

◆ Foam board has been around since 1957 (when the Monsanto Company sold it as Fome-Cor) and was mostly used by the graphic arts industry.

◆ The foam inside foam board is made of polystyrene, a kind of plastic also used to make plastic forks, DVD cases, insulation, and disposable cups.

◆ Sandwich boards are advertisements made of two printed boards with straps that a person can wear over his or her shoulders. One board hangs on the front, the other on the back.

Thaumatrope Name Spinner

This toy was all the rage during Victorian times . . . and you know how much fun those wacky Victorians were! Okay, so they were kind of a drag, but this little spinner is a bully good toy—that's Victorian slang for awesome.

MATERIALS
poster board ▪ ruler ▪ marker ▪ scissors ▪ hole punch
▪ two rubber bands

Cut poster board into two 4 x 6 inch pieces.

Stack the two pieces together so the edges are lined up. Now punch a hole on one short end of the cards, making it centered along the edge. Stick a rubber band through the hole and pull one loop through the other. Tug the rubber band so it's secure against the cards.

Punch a hole and loop a rubber band through it on the other end of the cards. Now you have rubber band loop handles on either side of the cards.

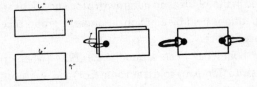

In large letters in the center of one side of the cards, write every other letter of your name, leaving a space for each missing letter. For example, because my name is Heather, my card would look like this: H _ A _ H _ R.

Hold the cards by the rubber bands and flip them over so the blank side of the cards is facing you. (Note: The letters on the side facing away from you will be upside down.) Hold the cards up to the light and lightly mark the blank spaces between the letters showing through the cards. Fill in the missing letters, right side up. For example, mine would look like this: _ E _ T _ E.

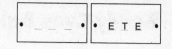

Hold the rubber bands in your fingers and twirl the cards to see your full name.

EXTRA FUN

◆ Instead of using your name, draw two incomplete pictures. (For example, on one side draw a boat. On the other side draw a person paddling.) When you're finished with the drawings, turn one upside down and face them away from each other. Attach the rubber bands and flip the cards to see the whole picture.

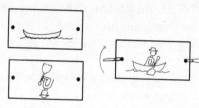

FUN FACT

When you spin a thaumatrope, your brain thinks it sees the images on both sides at the same time. This blending is called persistence of vision.

Beady Eyes Balancer

History lesson: This is the kind of travel toy kids played with on road trips before there were handheld electronic games. Seriously old-school.

MATERIALS
poster board ▪ two round transparent plastic container lids*
▪ markers ▪ scissors ▪ glue stick ▪ two round beads**
▪ masking tape

* Note: The lids have to be see-through for this to work. They also have to be circular and have a small rim around the outside so when you put them together, there's space for the balls to roll around inside.

** Note: Any small spherical object that rolls easily will work (such as marbles, beads, or ball bearings). The trick is to find the right size to roll around inside the two conjoined lids.

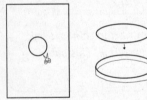

With a marker, outline the shape of a lid onto the poster board, then cut it out, being sure to cut on the inside of the line so that the poster board circle will fit inside the lid. You may need to trim it to make it fit.

Use markers to draw a face on the poster board, then cut out small circles from the face (or use a hole punch) for the center of the eyes so that the beads will get caught in them when they roll over the eyes.

Glue the poster board face to the inside of one lid.
    Put the beads on top of the poster board.
    Lay the other lid on top of the first one so that the rims come together.

Cut four small pieces of masking tape and secure the lids together at the twelve o'clock, three o'clock, six o'clock, and nine o'clock positions.

Run a long piece of masking tape around the outside edge of the rims to join them securely.

Hold the lids and roll the beads around until both stop in the eye holes.

EXTRA FUN

◆ Make a baseball game instead of a face to put inside the lids. Make holes at home plate, first base, second base, and third base. Shake the lid and see where your ball lands.

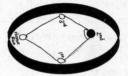

Cutout Dress-Up Dolls

Fashionistas-in-training will love having their own workshop for designing new clothes.

MATERIALS
poster board ■ pencil ■ scissors ■ colored pencils ■ drawing paper

Draw the outline of a person about 8 inches tall on the poster board. If you don't feel comfortable drawing your own doll, cut out or trace the template on page 212 so you can transfer it to your poster board. Once you have the person drawn on the poster board, carefully cut it out.

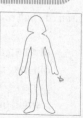

Petunia

Color in the face, hair, and underclothes on your paper doll then give him or her a name.

Place the doll on top of drawing paper. Follow the outline of the doll to make clothes. Add tabs to the tops and sides of the clothing.

Use colored pencils to color in the clothes.

Cut out the clothing, being sure to cut around the tabs.

Dress your doll by putting the clothes on and folding the tabs around the doll.

EXTRA FUN

◆ Make more dolls and put on a fashion show or have a party.

Misfit Marionettes

You can pull the strings to make this weird and wonderful dancer boogie.

MATERIALS
old magazines ■ scissors ■ poster board ■ glue stick ■ hole punch ■ ¼-inch circular reinforcement labels ■ sewing needle ■ small prong paper fasteners ■ thread or embroidery floss

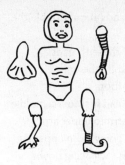

Using old magazines, cut out interesting animal or human body parts (heads, bodies, arms, legs, tails). Then glue a head and body onto the poster board so they fit together.

Next, glue the arms, legs, or other appendages separately to the poster board, so they are not touching one another.

When the glue is dry, cut out the head/body and each appendage.

Use the hole punch to make holes on each shoulder, upper arm, hip, upper leg, and lower leg. Then attach a circular reinforcement label around each hole. (This step is optional, but it will help your creature last longer.)

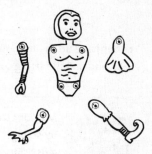

Over the top of the holes on the upper arms and upper legs, poke a needle through the reinforcement label and poster board. Also poke a hole in the top of the head.

Attach all the appendages to the back of the body with the prong paper fasteners. (Note: The tiny needle holes you made in the arms and legs will be behind the body.)

Thread the needle and bring it through the hole in one upper arm. Tie a knot and trim off the extra thread. Gently pull the thread

across the back of the marionette and through the hole in the other arm. You want the thread to be taut, but not tight. Tie a knot and trim the thread. Do the same for the upper legs.

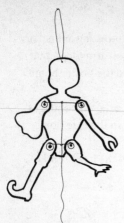

Next, cut two long pieces of thread (about double the length of your creature).

Use the needle to pull one of these threads through the hole in the head and tie the ends together so you create one long loop.

Tie the other long piece of thread first to the middle of the thread going from upper arm to upper arm, then to the middle of the thread going from upper leg to upper leg. The rest of the thread will hang down below the legs. This is the pull string.

Either hang up the marionette or hold it up by the top loop and pull the string to make your creature dance.

FUN FACT

Marionettes are puppets controlled by strings. They've been around at least since ancient Egyptian times.

No-Sew Butterfly Wings

No need for needle and thread to make these simple butterfly wings that are great for flitting among the flowers.

MATERIALS
poster board ▪ markers ▪ ruler ▪ scissors ▪ 12 x 12 inch square of felt ▪ glue ▪ string or tape measure ▪ six to ten large rubber bands ▪ stapler ▪ glitter

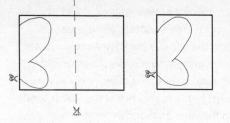

Decide how large you want your butterfly wings to be. Cut the poster board in half to make two large wings, or cut it into quarters to make smaller wings. On one piece of the poster board, draw a butterfly wing. Cut out the wing, then trace it on the other piece of poster board and cut that out, too.

Cut two 6 x 6 inch felt squares. Fold one square in half side to side. On the folded edge, measure down 1 inch from the top. Use a ruler to draw a straight line from the top outer corner to that mark, then cut along the line. Repeat on the bottom. When you unfold the felt it should look like the illustration. Cut the other piece of felt to match exactly. These pieces will hold the wings together so they can flap.

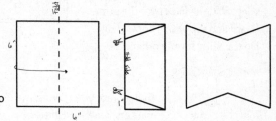

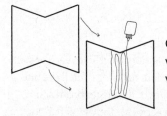

Cover the center 2 inches of one piece of felt with glue. Lay the other piece on top. Cover with a heavy book and let dry completely.

Use a string or tape measure to measure from the top of your butterfly person's shoulder, around the front, to the back of the armpit. Loop rubber bands together to form two chains this long.

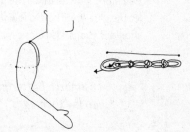

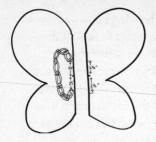

Find the center of the inside edge of one wing. Measure up 2½ inches and staple one end of one rubber band chain to this mark. Measure down 2½ inches from the center and staple the other end of the rubber band chain to this mark. (Now you will have 5 inches between the ends of the rubber band chain.) Do the same on the other wing.

Lay the joined felt pieces on the workspace. Fold one of the top flaps of felt back and cover the inner surfaces of the bottom and top flaps with glue. Insert a wing between the flaps so that the felt will cover the staples where the rubber bands are attached to the wing. Fold the flaps over the poster board and top with a book to dry. Do the same for the other side.

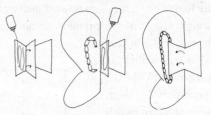

To decorate your wings, make pretty designs with markers, glue, and glitter.

EXTRA FUN

◆ Use ¼ yard of felt and fabric glue to make fancier wings. Trace each poster board wing twice onto the felt so you have four felt wings. Cut these out. Use fabric glue to attach the felt to both sides of the poster board and let the glue dry. Then follow the directions above for the center flap and shoulder straps. Use fabric markers and fabric glue with glitter to decorate.

FUN FACT

Monarch butterflies migrate nearly three thousand miles to lay their eggs.

Geo Board

Make lots of geometric designs with this simple pushpin and rubber band board, which is also a great travel toy for long car trips or airplane rides.

MATERIALS
foam board with ½-inch grid lines ▪ utility knife ▪ glue ▪ duct tape ▪ pushpins ▪ rubber bands (lots of colors, widths, and sizes work nicely)

Cut two 13 x 13 inch squares of foam board. With the grids facing out, glue the pieces back-to-back. Set aside to dry.

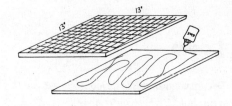

When the board is dry, use strips of duct tape to reinforce the bond, creating a ½-inch frame around the edges of the board.

Next, insert a pushpin every 1 inch to form a grid. Once you have the grid established, lift the pins one at a time, put a dot of glue around the hole, then push the pin back down. Set aside to dry.

Use rubber bands to make different shapes and designs on the pushpin grid.

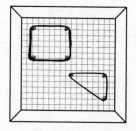

EXTRA FUN

◆ Try making three-sided triangles, four-sided squares and rectangles, five-sided pentagons, six-sided hexagons, and eight-sided octagons.

◆ Overlap different shapes to make interesting designs.

> **FUN FACT** Geo *stands for "geometry," which is the mathematical study of shapes first written down by a Greek dude named Euclid.*

Loom

Dream weaver, this little loom will get you through the night (and you'll even have a pot holder when you're done).

> **MATERIALS**
> foam board with ½-inch grid lines ▪ utility knife ▪ glue ▪ duct tape ▪ pushpins ▪ yarn (at least two colors) ▪ jumbo craft sticks (one for each color of yarn you use)

To Build the Loom

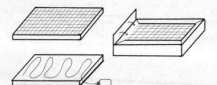

Cut out two 8 x 8 inch squares of foam core. With the grids facing out, glue the foam core back-to-back. Use strips of duct tape to reinforce the bond, creating a ½-inch frame around the edges of the board.

When the board is dry, insert the pushpins every ½ inch in a line along the top and the bottom of the loom. Once you have the line of pushpins established, lift the pins one at a time, put a dot of glue around the hole, then push the pin back down. Set aside to dry.

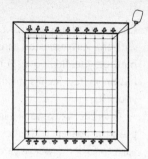

To String the Loom

Choose one color of yarn. Tie an end around the top left pushpin.

Pull the yarn down and loop it around (from the outside toward the inside) the bottom left pushpin.

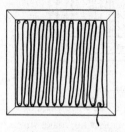

Pull the yarn back up and loop it around the next pushpin at the top.

Continue this way, looping the yarn down and up, around the pushpins, until you reach the bottom right pushpin. Tie the yarn off and trim the end, leaving a few inches for a tail. (This yarn is called the warp.)

Take one jumbo craft stick and work it in between the warp yarn by going over, under, over, under, until the stick traverses the width of the warp. Push it to the top of the loom. (This is called the beater.)

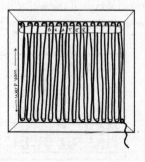

To Weave

Cut 1 yard of each color of yarn you want to use. Tie one end of each yarn around the center of a jumbo craft stick. Wrap the yarn around the craft stick, leaving about 12 inches free. (These colors are called the weft.)

Choose a color to start. At the bottom of the loom, weave the craft stick with the yarn attached through the warp yarns, using the same over, under method you did above. Pull the yarn all the way through until the free end has only a few inches sticking out. Tie this end to the tail of the warp yarn you left.

Give the weave yarn a little tug to make sure it's taut, but not tight. Now push the beater (craft stick) that's inside your warp yarn down onto the weft yarn to tuck the weave yarn gently against the bottom. Return the beater to its place at the top.

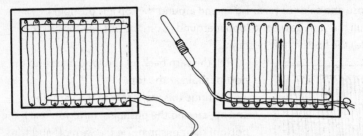

Unwind some of the weft yarn from the crawft stick. Weave back through the warp, making sure to loop the weft yarn around the last warp yarn. In other words, if the weft came out on top of the last warp string, make sure when you turn around, you put the weft under that string, and vice versa.

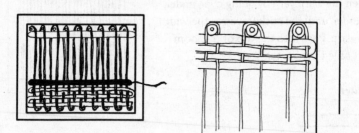

Continue this way, weaving one way, pushing the weave yarn down with the beater, then weaving the other way. Change colors whenever you want by trimming the end of the weave yarn, leaving a tail to knot around the outside warp string. When you switch colors, tie the new color onto the outside warp string before you start.

When the weave yarn gets near the top, remove the beater and use your fingers to push the weave down snugly against the row below.

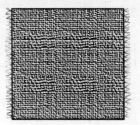

At the end, tie off the last piece of weft yarn on the outside warp string. Remove the warp yarns from the pushpins to see your woven masterpiece!

EXTRA FUN

◆ Make a larger loom to create bigger pieces of woven fabric.

◆ Sew squares of your woven fabric together to make a blanket for your favorite stuffed animal.

FUN FACT

Most cloth was woven at home by women until automatic looms were invented in the early eighteenth century.

Stacking Box Face Puzzle

This is a versatile puzzle based on an old toy catalog favorite called Ole Charlie Million Faces.

> **MATERIALS**
> foam board with ½-inch grid lines ▪ utility knife ▪ ruler
> ▪ markers ▪ masking and/or transparent tape

For this project you will create ten small cubed-shaped boxes using the pattern and instructions below. However, if you happen to have ten small wooden cube-shaped blocks lying around, and you want to paint them white instead of sitting around making boxes all afternoon, that would work, too.

To Make the Boxes

Use the utility knife to cut out ten pieces of foam board that follow the pattern shown here, or use the template on page 213. (Note: The picture below shows an exaggeration of the grid lines, which are very faint on the foam board.)

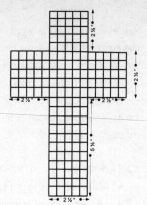

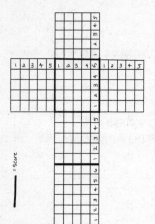

With the grid lines as a guide, use the utility knife and the edge of the ruler to gently score (cut halfway through the foam) along the fold lines marked below.

With the grid lines facing up, decorate the boxes so that each box is for a different feature of the face and each side of the box has a different picture on it. For example, one box will be for noses. There are six sides to a box, so draw six different kinds of noses, one on each side. Remember the grid lines are very faint and will recede from view once you've decorated the sides. (Note: Leave one row of the grid blank on the largest of the sides, as shown.)

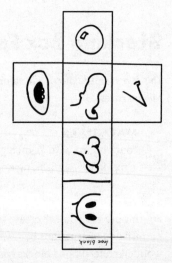

Your ten boxes should be decorated as follows:

- one box: hats and/or hair
- two boxes: eyes
- two boxes: ears*
- one box: noses*
- two boxes: half mouths (see below)
- two boxes: blank, for the base

* Note: You may want to make
the two eye and the two ear boxes
match. For example, if you draw a
big blue eye on a side of one eye
box, draw the same eye on a side
of the other eye box.

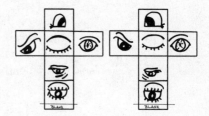

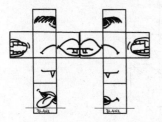

For the mouth boxes, lay the boxes next to
one another and draw a full mouth, half on
each box.

Now fold each box as shown below, with the facial features facing out.
Secure each seam on the inside of the box with masking or transparent tape.

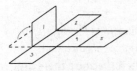

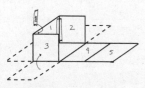

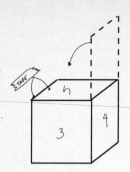

Once you fold the last side down, trim any excess that hangs over, then use transparent tape on the outside of the box.

When all the boxes are complete, stack them up to create a face like this:

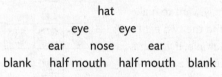

```
                hat
            eye      eye
        ear      nose      ear
   blank   half mouth   half mouth   blank
```

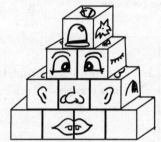

Rearrange the blocks for new funny faces.

There are 1,679,616 possible combinations for different faces with this puzzle. In order to figure this out, you would take 6 x 6 x 6 x 6 x 6 x 6 x 6 x 6 (because there are six sides of eight cubes).

RUBBER BAND PROJECTS

BEFORE I STARTED making toys, I never noticed how many rubber bands are lurking in our world. Now I seem to find them everywhere—on fruits, vegetables, and flowers, around the mail and newspapers, inside packaging, and in my hair! They're such nifty little creations that can do everything from binding to propelling to singing.

FACTS ABOUT RUBBER BANDS

- Rubber bands are made from latex, which comes from rubber trees. First the latex is collected from the tree, then it's purified, squeezed into slabs, and sent to factories to be processed into rubber.
- The Mayans were already using rubber to make waterproof shoes and bottles when Christopher Columbus stumbled upon them.
- Vulcanized rubber (the manufactured stuff we use today) was discovered in 1839 by accident when Charles Goodyear accidentally left some natural rubber with sulfur and lead on top of a warm stove.
- In the mid 1800s, Thomas Hancock cut up a rubber bottle to make the first rubber bands, which were used to hold up stockings and pants.
- The U.S. Postal Service is the biggest consumer of rubber bands in the world. Workers use them to organize the mail as they sort it.

Chair Leg Catapult

Intruders! Steady the catapult. Ready. Aim. Fire away!

MATERIALS

small round disposable plastic container ▪ hole punch ▪ long skinny stick (optional) ▪ chair ▪ two to eight rubber bands ▪ Ping-Pong ball

Punch two holes, directly across from one another, near the top rim of the plastic container. (To make sure they line up, punch one, then stick something long and thin through the hole, such as a chopstick, pencil, or skewer, and mark where it hits the other side.)

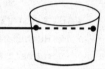

To determine how many rubber bands you'll need for each side of the catapult, place the container on the floor midway between two chair legs. Lay rubber bands from one side of the container to the near leg, then take one rubber band away.

Now make two rubber band chains, linking the rubber bands for each side as show.

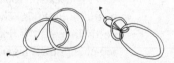

Slip one end of a rubber band chain through one of the holes on the outside of the container. Pull the first rubber band in the chain partway through and up, then pull the opposite end of the chain through the loop and tighten.

Repeat this process for the other side.

Slip the free ends of your rubber band chains over the bottoms of the two chair legs. Lie on the floor behind the chair. Reach through the legs and pull the container toward you.

Place your Ping-Pong ball inside the container and let 'er rip!

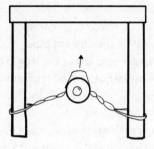

EXTRA FUN

◆ Chair leg catapults are excellent defense systems for secret cave dwellers (page 117) and the occupants of a castle with a drawbridge (page 42) and can only be countered by mini-marshmallow poppers (page 4).

FUN FACT

Catapults were invented as weapons to hurl objects at enemy forces. Now that they've gone out of favor, people have found different uses for them. The craziest use might be the "human catapult," which tosses people high into the air for fun.

Come Back, Ralphie Rolling Dog

Ralphie is a very well-trained dog who always comes back. If you want the technical explanation for why this works, we'll have to discuss potential and kinetic energy, so maybe it's better to say that Ralphie is simply an obedient little fellow.

||||||||| MATERIALS ||||||||||||||||||||||||||||||||||||||||||||||||||||||||||||||||

can with a plastic lid* ▪ marker ▪ hammer ▪ nail ▪ construction paper ▪ scissors ▪ transparent tape ▪ two rubber bands (one small and one larger one, about the length of the can) ▪ two small paper clips ▪ metal nut or washers from the toolbox

* Note: The kind of can I'm thinking of is usually made from aluminum or heavy cardboard and has a metal bottom and a plastic lid, like the kind peanuts, coffee, or bread crumbs come in. I like small cans but you can use any size; just adjust the size of the rubber bands and use more washers or a heavier nut for the weight on the inside.

Remove the lid from the can. Flip the can upside down and put the lid over the bottom of the can. Use your marker to make a dot in the center of the lid. Place the nail on the dot and give it a few good whacks with the hammer to make a hole in both the lid and the bottom of the can. Remove the lid and set aside.

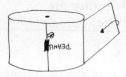

Cut a piece of brown (or other color) construction paper so that it will wrap around the can. Tape it securely.

Slip a paper clip onto the larger rubber band. From the outside, stick the free end of the rubber band through the hole in the bottom of the can (be careful: the edges of the hole might be jagged). From the inside, pull the rubber band so the paper clip is flat against the bottom outside of the can.

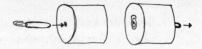

Cut the smaller rubber band so it's no longer a loop. Tie one end around the center of the larger rubber band inside the can, then slip the free end through the metal nut. This will be a weight. (If you don't have a nut, use a few metal washers or something else you can hang from the larger rubber band to form a weight.)

Slip the other paper clip over the free end of the rubber band. Poke the paper clip through the hole in the lid (from the inside of the lid to the outside) and tug on the rubber band until the paper clip goes all the way through.

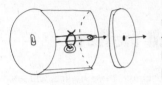

Attach the lid to the can and tug on the rubber band until the paper clip lies flat against the outside of the lid. The rubber band should be taut between the bottom of the can and the lid, with the weight hanging in the middle.

Lay the can on its side so it will roll. Use the marker to draw a dog's face and front legs on one side of the can. Then spin the can around and draw a tail and hind legs on the opposite side.

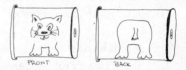

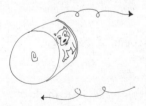

Roll the can across a smooth flat surface. As the can slows, say, "Come back, Ralphie!" and your dog will roll back to you every time! Good dog, Ralphie.

EXTRA FUN

◆ Use different-sized cans, rubber bands, and weights to make more rolling creatures (such as a Tasmanian devil, a hedgehog, or your own weird monster) or simply decorate your can with stickers.

◆ See which rolling creature goes the farthest before returning, which one is easiest to push, which one is the most stubborn.

FUN FACT

The can always rolls back because as the rubber band inside the can gets twisted, it stores energy. Once it can't wind anymore, it begins to unwind, converting the stored energy into kinetic energy, which sends the can rolling backward again.

Rubber Band and Pencil Mallet

If you have any natural-born drummers in your house, these mallets will keep them busy, but since they're made from rubber bands they can't do much damage (except maybe to your eardrums).

MATERIALS
about twenty rubber bands ▪ unsharpened wooden pencil with eraser

Wrap one rubber band at a time around the eraser end of the pencil.

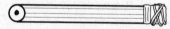

Continue wrapping until you have a 3-inch-diameter mallet head made of rubber bands. (Depending on the size of your materials, this will take about twenty rubber bands.)

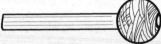

You will see the tip of the eraser sticking out from among the rubber bands.

- ◆ Make another one for a matching set to play your tubular drums (page 26) or double-sided drum (page 175)!
- ◆ Make all the musical instruments in this book with your friends and form your own band.

Violin

The rubber band strings on this clever violin resonate to give you different notes when you pluck them.

MATERIALS

plastic container from travel baby wipes (empty, clean, and dry)
■ four rubber bands of different thicknesses ■ masking tape
■ 12-inch dowel with one flat side ■ cardboard tube from a dry cleaner hanger* ■ ruler ■ pencil ■ scissors ■ glue

* Note: You can use any two round, 4-inch-long objects, like crayons, small pencils, a cut chopstick, or birthday candles, instead of the dry cleaner tube.

Remove the pop-up lid from the wipes box so there is a hole in the center of the top.

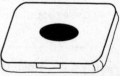

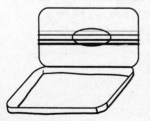

Open the box and place four rubber bands lengthwise around the top, starting with the thickest band farthest to one side and ending with the thinnest band farthest to the other side.

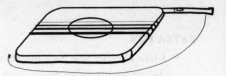

Close the box and secure it shut with tape.

Lay the flat side of the dowel lengthwise centered on the back of the box. Use masking tape to secure it to the box.

Cut the cardboard dry cleaning hanger tube into two 4-inch pieces. Put a line of glue on the bottom of each (or two other round, 4-inch-long objects) and slip them under the rubber bands, just to either side of the hole. Press down to affix the pieces to the box. This will allow the "strings" to resonate.

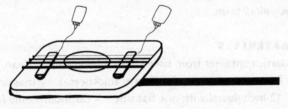

Pluck out a tune!

EXTRA FUN

◆ Make all the musical instruments in this book with your friends and form your own band.

◆ Use a chopstick or other long, thin stick as a pretend bow.

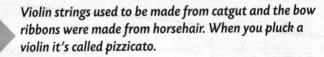

> **FUN FACT**
>
> *Violin strings used to be made from catgut and the bow ribbons were made from horsehair. When you pluck a violin it's called pizzicato.*

Shoe Box Guitar

You can make your own six-string gee-tar with a shoe box and a cardboard tube.

> **MATERIALS**
> kid-sized shoe box with lid ▪ paper towel tube (or a 12-inch length from a wrapping paper or mailing tube) ▪ marker ▪ ruler ▪ utility knife ▪ glue ▪ masking tape ▪ six rubber bands of different thicknesses ▪ cardboard tube from a dry cleaner hanger* ▪ scissors

* Note: You can use any two round, 4-inch-long objects, like crayons, small pencils, a cut chopstick, or birthday candles, instead.

Take the lid off the box and set it aside.
Put one end of the large cardboard tube against one of the short sides of the box, so that it is centered and it lines up with the bottom of the box. Trace around the circle.

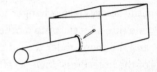

Use a ruler to draw four straight lines bisecting the circle, crossing in the center (so it looks like an asterisk). Cut along these lines with the utility knife. (Hint: Flip the box upside down and hold it steady with one hand while you start from the outside of the circle and cut inward, using a gently sawing motion so you don't rip the box.)

When all the lines are cut, gently push the points inside the box then push the paper towel tube through the hole until it hits the opposite side.

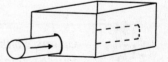

Run a line of glue beneath the cardboard tube and press it down on the bottom of the box.

Use small pieces of masking tape to secure the points of the circle you cut against the cardboard tube.

Secure the rest of the tube with long pieces of tape going over the tube and attaching to either side on the bottom of the box.

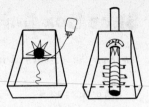

Draw a large oval in the center of the lid. Use the utility knife to cut out the oval, then put the lid on the box and set it so the neck points away from you.

Stretch the rubber bands around the length of the box, starting with the thickest band farthest left down to the thinnest band on the right side,

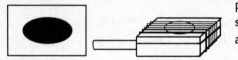

positioning three bands on one side of the cardboard tube neck and three on the other.

Cut the dry cleaner hanger tube into two 4-inch pieces. Put a line of glue on one side of each (or two other round, 4-inch-long objects) and slip them under the rubber bands, just to either side of the hole. Press down to affix the pieces to the box. This will allow the "strings" to resonate.

Strum or pluck out a tune.

EXTRA FUN

- ◆ Guitars can be plucked or strummed. The plastic tab from a bread bag makes an excellent pick.
- ◆ Make all the musical instruments in this book with your friends and form your own band.

FUN FACT

Guitars, which can be acoustic or electric and have from four to eighteen strings, are used in a variety of musical styles, such as jazz, flamenco, blues, country, mariachi, rock, pop, and classical.

Banjo

Banjos are different from guitars because they have a resonator head beneath the strings, made here with a Tyvek envelope.

MATERIALS

heavy-duty paper bowl ▪ paper towel tube ▪ marker ▪ ruler ▪ utility knife ▪ glue ▪ masking tape ▪ Tyvek envelope ▪ scissors ▪ hole punch ▪ five rubber bands of different thicknesses ▪ ten pony beads ▪ cardboard tube from a dry cleaner hanger*

* Note: You can use any two round, 4-inch-long objects, like crayons, small pencils, a cut chopstick, or birthday candles, instead.

Flip the bowl upside down and hold one end of the paper towel tube against its side so it lines up with the bottom (which is the bowl's rim). Use a marker to trace around the tube on the side of the bowl.

Use a ruler to draw four straight lines bisecting the circle, crossing in the center (so it looks like an asterisk). Cut along these lines with the utility knife. (Hint: Start from the outside of the circle and cut inward, using a gently sawing motion so you don't rip the bowl.)

When all the lines are cut, flip the bowl over and gently push the points inside the bowl, then push the paper towel tube through the hole until it hits the opposite side. Run a line of glue beneath the cardboard tube and press it down on the bottom of the bowl.

Use small pieces of masking tape to secure the points of the circle you cut against the cardboard tube.

Secure the tube with long pieces of tape going over the tube and attaching to either side on the bottom of the bowl.

Cut open the Tyvek envelope and trim off a large piece with no seams. Turn the bowl upside down on the Tyvek and trace around it. Then draw another circle around this one that is wider than the first by 1 inch all around. (Don't sweat this; it doesn't have to be perfect. If you're doing it freehand, you can use a ruler to measure out 1 inch from the first circle, in eight different directions, making a dot each time. Connect these dots to draw the outside circle.)

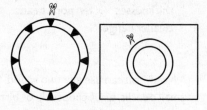

Cut around the larger circle. Then, every 2 inches around the circle, cut a V-shaped notch that ends at the smaller circle to make tabs.

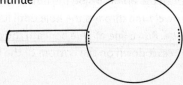

Center the bowl upside down on the Tyvek. Secure the tabs, one at a time, around the bowl with masking tape. (Hint: Tape a tab, then do the one opposite it so you can pull the Tyvek head taut.) Once all the tabs are taped down, flip the banjo over.

Mark five dots across the rim of the bowl/head that are centered over the cardboard tube neck. They should be about ⅛ inch apart and ¼ inch from the edge. Use your ruler as a guide to mark five dots opposite these on the other end of the bowl.

Line up your hole punch over the first dot and punch a hole through the Tyvek head and the rim of the bowl. Continue punching until you have ten holes (five on each side of the bowl).

Snip open the five rubber bands. Knot a pony bead over one end of each. On the neck end of the banjo head, reach under the rim of the bowl and slip the free end of the rubber band through the first hole. Pull the rubber

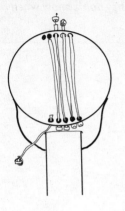

band up through the hole so that it comes out on top of the head and the bead fits snug between the rim of the bowl and top of the cardboard tube neck. (If you're using different sizes, with the banjo neck pointing away from you, arrange the rubber bands so the thickest is farthest to your left and the thinnest is farthest to your right.) Repeat for each hole.

Once all the rubber bands are through the neck end holes, pull each one across the head and slip through their opposite holes. Tie a pony bead on this end of each rubber band to finish the strings and hold them in place.

Cut the dry cleaner hanger tube into two 4-inch pieces. Put a line of glue on each (or two other round, 4-inch-long objects) and slip them under the rubber bands at the top and bottom of the banjo

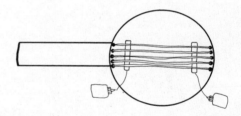

head. Press down to affix the pieces to the head. This will allow the "strings" to resonate when you pluck your first tune!

EXTRA FUN

- ◆ Use the plastic tab from a bread bag as a pick to pluck or strum your banjo.
- ◆ Make all the musical instruments in this book with your friends and form your own band.

FUN FACT

Here's an old bluegrass banjo joke for you: How can you tell if banjo players are at your door? They can't find the key, the knocking speeds up, and they don't know when to come in.

SPOOL PROJECTS

SPOOLS HAVE LONG been a favorite for home toy makers, partly because they were readily available when people used to do a lot of sewing at home, and partly because they have an ingenious design perfect for wheels and propellers. If you sew, you'll likely have some empty spools lying around that can be put to good use here. But even if you aren't whipping up quilts in your spare time, you can pick up empty wooden spools at craft stores.

FACTS ABOUT SPOOLS
- Barthélemy Thimmonier, a Frenchman who invented the first functional sewing machine, was nearly killed when a mob of angry tailors set his factory on fire. They were afraid they'd lose their jobs if sewing machines caught on.
- On modern sewing machines, both a spool and a bobbin (which is a shorter, small sort of spool) hold thread. The spool goes on top of the machine and the bobbin goes beneath the needle. The machine takes thread from both the spool and the bobbin to create a top and bottom stitch on the fabric.
- Stacked thread is wound straight on a spool and comes off the side of the spool when sewing. Crossover thread is wound in a diamond pattern so that the thread comes off the top of the spool.
- Artist Devorah Sperber re-creates masterwork paintings, such as the *Mona Lisa*, with thousands of spools of thread. Her large, pixelated images, which can be 10 x 10 feet, are installed upside down with a small viewing sphere in front of them that condenses the image and turns it right side up so the viewer sees what appears to be a miniature version of the original painting.

Rolling Dogs

Here's a simple but adorable homemade push- or pull-along toy.

MATERIALS
flimsy paper plate ▪ markers or crayons ▪ scissors ▪ hole punch ▪ drinking straw ▪ two small empty spools

Fold the paper plate in half. Draw the outline of the profile of a dog's head and body on the plate so that the fold will run down the center of the dog's back (or use the template on page 214). Cut out and decorate your dog with markers or crayons.

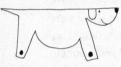

Hold the front legs together and punch a hole in them ¼ inch from the bottom. Do the same for the back legs.

Cut the drinking straw in half. Slip one piece of the straw through a hole in the front leg. Put a spool over the straw, then put the straw through the hole in the other leg.

Even out the straw and trim so ½ inch sticks out from the each leg. Repeat this process for the back.

Now your dog will stand up on the spools. Give him a little push and watch him roll!

EXTRA FUN

◆ Make other four-legged creatures (cats, cows, horses, etc.).

- Make two and have races (which is faster, the tortoise or the hare?).
- Turn this into a pull toy by poking a small hole on the neck fold with one leg of the scissors. Cut a long piece of string, tie a knot in one end, and put the other end through the hole (starting on the outside top of the animal). Pull the string under the animal and attach with transparent tape on the crease underneath the face.

Sneaky Windup Mouse

This little critter (based on an old-fashioned toy called a spool tank that kids used to make out of wooden spools, sticks, and rubber bands) will stop and start then scurry across the floor in a flash.

MATERIALS

two drinking straws ■ empty spool ■ ruler ■ markers
■ scissors ■ small paper clip ■ rubber band ■ masking tape
■ thin, flat piece of foam (such as from the top of an egg carton or a plate)* ■ hole punch

* Note: Foam works great for this project because it's so light, but if you don't have any around the house, you can use thin cardboard.

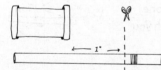

Trim one straw so it's 1 inch longer than the spool.

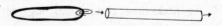

Slip the paper clip over the rubber band. Push the paper clip all the way through the straw, keeping a bit of the rubber band peeking out of the other end. (You may need to use a toothpick, skewer, or another paper clip to push it through.)

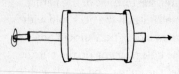

Poke the straw (rubber band end first) through the hole in the spool so that the paper clip lies flat against the side of the spool and the long end of the straw sticks out the other end.

Secure the paper clip to the spool with a bit of masking tape.

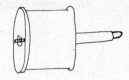

On the foam, draw a 3-inch mouse, the bottom of which is flat (or use the template on page 215). Cut out the mouse then punch a hole in the front.

Slip the mouse over the straw sticking out of the spool. Cut a 2½-inch piece of the other straw and slide it through the loop of rubber band that's sticking out of the straw (next to the mouse). This the winder.

Twist the winder many, many times until the rubber band is taut inside the straw. You have to wind the rubber band really tight to make this work. Sometimes the rubber band will be uncooperative at first. A good snap of the winder usually gets things going. Put the spool on the floor with one end of the winder touching the ground. Watch your mouse stop and start and scurry!

EXTRA FUN

◆ Make other critters (cats, dogs, gerbils, etc.) or different kinds of vehicles (cars, trains, trucks, etc.) to attach to the straw.

FUN FACT

Windup toys have been around for at least five hundred years. In 1509, inventor Leonardo da Vinci made a life-sized windup lion to welcome the French king, Louis XII, to Italy.

Helicopter

A foam take-out container is the perfect thing for this helicopter with a windup propeller.

MATERIALS

burger-sized foam take-out container (clamshell type)* ▪ permanent markers ▪ ruler ▪ utility knife ▪ thin cardboard (such as from a cereal or cracker box) ▪ scissors ▪ hole punch ▪ masking tape ▪ four drinking straws ▪ two empty spools ▪ flat piece of foam (such as from the top of an egg carton or a plate) ▪ paper clip ▪ rubber band

* Note: You could also use a paperboard sandwich container, or more eco-friendly sugarcane varieties, if it's not too greasy from your food.

Close the take-out container (aka your helicopter) and flip it upside down. Lightly mark the front of the helicopter, making sure the flap that holds the container closed is on one side. On the bottom surface, mark two straight 1-inch lines along one side edge (perpendicular to the front of the helicopter), ½ inch away from the edge; make one line start ½ inch from the

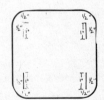

front end and the other ½ inch from the back end. Repeat along the opposite side edge. Use the utility knife to cut slits along these four lines.

Measure the distance between the slits that are on opposite sides from one another. Then cut two 1-inch-wide strips of cardboard, the lengths of which are the distance between the slits plus 3 inches. For example, if the distance between the slits is 3 inches, your cardboard piece would measure 6 inches (3 plus 3).

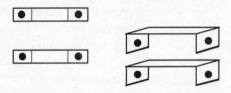
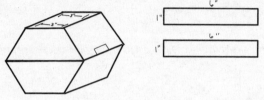

Score the strips crosswise 1½ inch from each end and punch a hole ¼ inch from each end. Fold the strips along the scores.

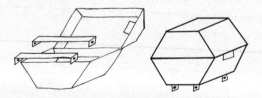

Open the container and slip the cardboard strips into the slits so that the ends with the holes stick out the bottom. Secure the strips with tape against the inside bottom of the container.

Insert a straw through one hole like an axle through a hub. Slide a spool over the straw, then slip the straw through the opposite hole. Trim the ends of the straw so that only ½ inch sticks out beyond the hubs. Repeat with the other straw and spools to form two axles, each with a spool wheel.

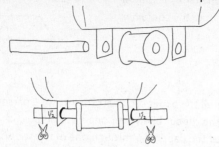

At each end of both straws cut a slit through the top and bottom of the straw to split the end in half. Fold each half back and tape it against the wheel hub to hold the axle in place.

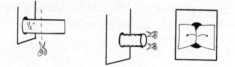

Open the container again. From the inside, poke a small hole in the center of the top and bottom of the container. (The hole should be about the diameter of a straw. Make sure the holes line up exactly with one another when the container is closed.)

Trim a flat piece of foam into a 6 x 2½ inch rectangle to make the tail of the helicopter. Tape the front end of it to the inside back of the top of the container, and let the rear end stick out behind.

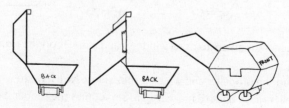

Now build the propeller by trimming two straws so they are 2 inches taller than the container (when closed).

Pull the paper clip apart so it forms a narrow S shape. Hook the rubber band over one side and push the opposite side of the paper clip through one of the straws, leaving the other end of the rubber band peeking out. (You may need to use a toothpick, skewer, or another paper clip to push it through all the way.) This straw is the propeller shaft. Then slip the other straw through the loop of the rubber band that's peeking out (on the opposite side from the paper clip.) This straw is the propeller.

Push the propeller shaft down through the hole in the top of the closed container and then continue through the hole in the bottom. Now place the paper clip that's sticking out of the straw flat against the bottom of the container. Secure it with tape.

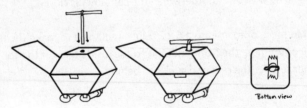

Bottom view

Use permanent markers to draw windows and a driver on the front of the container.

Wind up the propeller and watch it spin. (Note, you have to wind the propeller really tight to make it spin. Sometimes the rubber band is uncooperative at first; keep winding and give the propeller arm a few snaps to loosen the rubber band. Pretty soon it'll whiz right along.)

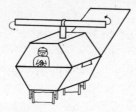

FUN FACT

The propeller, or rotor, on top of the helicopter provides lift, which is why helicopters take off straight up and can hover.

Fairy-Go-Round

Fairies are always looking for a good time and love to get dizzy. This spinning ride will keep them deliriously happy!

MATERIALS

two empty spools (with a hole that a knitting needle or chopstick can slide through easily) ▪ glue ▪ unwanted knitting needle ▪ toothpicks ▪ two rubber bands ▪ heavy-duty paper plate ▪ markers (optional) ▪ scissors ▪ 1 yard of string ▪ masking tape

Squirt a bit of glue into the center hole of one spool then slide it over the knitting needle, pushing it up to the knob end.

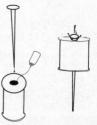

This spool must fit snugly against the needle, so use a few toothpicks as shims by sliding them in between the spool and needle, if necessary. Break off

the ends that stick out beyond the spool. Set aside to dry. (Note: The needle must not move inside this spool.)

Slide the second spool over the knitting needle. The needle must be able to spin freely inside this one.

Wind a rubber band tightly around the needle 3 inches from the pointed end.

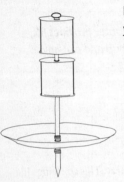

Decorate the top of the plate with markers if you want, then use one leg of the scissors to poke a small hole in the center of the plate.

With the plate facing up as if you were going to eat off it, poke the pointy end of the needle (with the spools on it) through the hole in the plate. Push the needle up until it's against the rubber band.

Wind the other rubber band tightly around the needle just below the plate. Now the plate should fit snugly between both rubber bands.

Tie the string around the top, glued-on spool and secure it with a bit of masking tape. Wind the string around the spool, leaving just a few inches to hold.

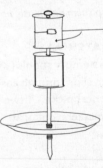

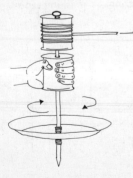

Stand the fairy-go-round up on the needle point and grasp the lower spool. Hold the string in your other hand and pull (keeping hold of the lower spool).

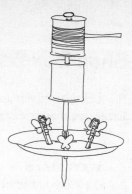

Watch your fairy-go-round spin!

EXTRA FUN

◆ Make clothespin fairies (page 61). Use a utility knife to cut small slits around the edge, just below the lip of the plate. Slide the end of the fairies into the slit so they stand up. Give your fairies a ride on their very own fairy-go-round.

◆ If you want to make a carousel, glue your favorite small plastic animals around the edge of the plate.

In sixteenth-century France, knights on horseback entertained royalty with games and tournaments called "carrousels." The horses wore elaborate costumes and sometimes the events were accompanied by music.

Shoe Box Baby Carriage

This is an updated version of a cigar box carriage from an early 1900s toy book. Since cigars have gone largely out of favor (cough, cough) this one uses a shoe box instead.

░░░░ **MATERIALS** ░░

5 x 7 inch kid-sized shoe box with lid (see note below for using other sizes)* ▪ pencil ▪ ruler ▪ scissors ▪ hole punch ▪ utility knife ▪ two drinking straws ▪ four empty spools ▪ transparent tape ▪ poster board

* Note: You can use any size shoe box for this if you follow the proportions given below.

To Make the Carriage

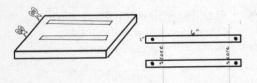

Cut two 1 x 6 inch strips from the shoe box lid. (Length of strip = width of the shoe box plus 1 inch.) Score the strips crosswise 1 inch from each end and punch a hole ¼ inch from each end.

Turn the box upside down and mark two straight 1-inch lines along one side edge, ½ inch away from the edge and parallel to it; make one line start 2 inches from the front end of the box and the other 2 inches from the back. Repeat along the other side edge. Use the utility knife to make slits along these four lines.

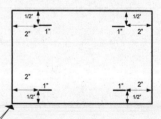

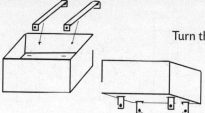

Turn the box right side up. Fold down the ends of the strips and slide them through the slits so the holes stick out the bottom.

Insert a straw through one hole like an axle through a hub. Slide two spools over the straw, then slip the straw through the opposite hole. Repeat with the other straw and spools to form two axles with two wheels each.

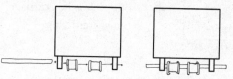

Trim the straws so that only a ½ inch sticks out beyond the hubs. At each end of both straws cut a slit through the top and bottom of the straw to split the end in half. Fold each half back and tape against the wheel hub to hold the axle in place.

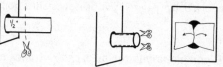

To Make the Hood

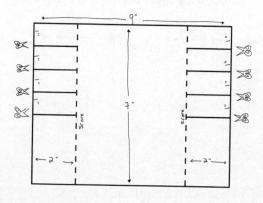

Cut a piece of poster board into a 7 x 9 inch rectangle. (Width of the box plus 2 inches x width of the box plus 4 inches.)

Then measure and mark the poster board as shown. Cut along the solid lines to create four 1-inch tabs on each side. Then score along the dotted lines.

Fold along the scored lines and begin to fold the tabs over one another, gathering the bottoms of the tabs together so that the top of the hood curves. Secure the tabs together with tape.

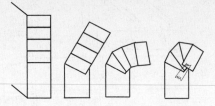

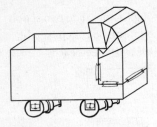

Wrap the hood piece around one end of the shoe box carriage. Secure with transparent tape.

EXTRA FUN

◆ Make a soft and cozy bed with dish towels, washcloths, or scraps of fabric.
◆ Give your sock baby (page 93) or no-sew T-shirt doll (page 115) a ride.

FUN FACT

Pram, perambulator, push chair, stroller, and baby buggy are other names for a baby carriage. Try saying the tongue twister "Rubber baby buggy bumpers" ten times really fast.

TYVEK PROJECTS

AS AN OFFICIAL craft nerd, I have to confess, I'm in love with Tyvek. You can staple, glue, or sew it. It's hard to tear but easy to cut. It's water resistant. You can paint it or use permanent markers to decorate it. And it's nontoxic (but that doesn't mean I'd let a tot chomp on it). Think you don't have any Tyvek lying around? Oh, but you do, my friend, you do. Those strange half-fabric/half-paper mailing envelopes are made from the stuff. Mosey on down to your local office supply store and ask the friendly clerk where she keeps the Tyvek envelopes. Or, if you happen to be at the post office, pick up a Priority Mail envelope or two.

FACTS ABOUT TYVEK

- Tyvek is a brand name for spunbonded olefin, a nonwoven fabric made of high-density polyethylene fibers that are spun then bound together by heat.
- Jim White, a researcher for DuPont, accidentally discovered Tyvek when he noticed white polyethylene fluff coming out of a pipe in a DuPont lab.
- Tyvek is used in envelopes, house wrap, coveralls, car covers, outdoor banners, ski tags, industrial packaging, and hospital scrubs, among other things.
- Artists use Tyvek to make beads, book jackets, paintings, dolls, and collages.

Pinwheel

Yeah, I know, we've all seen pinwheels before, but hear me out on this one . . . Most homemade pinwheels either fall apart in ten seconds or don't spin, sometimes both. This one will spin with the best of the store-bought kind and last through a nor'easter.

MATERIALS

Tyvek envelope ▪ ruler ▪ pencil ▪ scissors ▪ hole punch ▪ paper reinforcement circle (optional) ▪ wine cork ▪ bamboo skewer or wooden chopstick with a pointy end ▪ pushpin

Cut a piece of Tyvek into an 8 x 8 inch square. Lightly with pencil, label the corners A, B, C, and D in order around the square.

Fold corner A to corner C and make a crease. Open. Now fold corner B to corner D, make a crease, and open. Make a dot where the creases cross one another in the center of the square.

Next, measure ½ inch from the dot along each crease and make a mark. Cut from each corner tip toward the center, stopping at the ½-inch mark. Use the hole punch to make a hole in the center of the square.

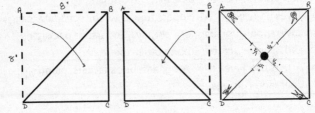

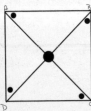

Punch a hole in the tip of the same outside corner on each of the four flaps, as marked.

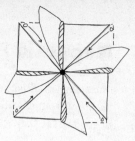

Fold the flaps with the holes at each corner in toward the center hole. If you happen to have some paper reinforcement circles around, press one over the top of the overlapping circles.

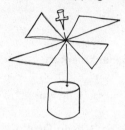

Put the sharp end of the pushpin through the overlapping circles, then press this into the center of the flat side of a cork. Don't push it in too far; you need a little room for the pinwheel to spin.

Push the sharp end of the bamboo skewer or chopstick into the bottom of the cork at the opposite end from the pushpin.

Blow!

EXTRA FUN

◆ After you've cut the pinwheel out, decorate it with permanent markers or paint. Mess around to find interesting patterns that look good when the pinwheel spins.

◆ Try making larger and smaller pinwheels.

FUN FACT

Pioneer kids played with homemade pinwheels carved out of wood.

Magnetic Fish and Fishing Pole

Most magnetic fishing toys don't use water. The fish lie around on the ground like, uh, um, fish out of water. This one is fun because the fish hang out in real, honest-to-goodness H₂O.

MATERIALS FOR THE FISH

Tyvek envelope ▪ scissors ▪ pencil ▪ permanent markers ▪ paper clip ▪ stapler

Cut the envelope open and fold it in half so the white side faces up. Draw a 3-inch fish. (See sample below or use the template on page 215.) Cut the fish out, going through both layers of Tyvek. Decorate the white side of both fish with permanent markers (first lay the two fish nose to nose to make sure the eyes and mouth you draw on both pieces line up.)

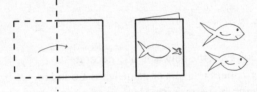

Lay one fish on your workspace with the print side facing up (and the decorated side facing down). Lay a paper clip in the center of the fish.

Put the other fish on top with the decorated side facing up. Staple around the edges.

MATERIALS FOR THE FISHING POLE

12-inch string ▪ 12-inch stick ▪ magnet you can tie onto a string

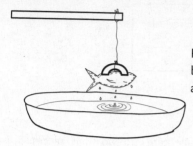

Tie one end of the string to one end of the stick.
Tie the magnet to the other end of the string.

Put your fish in some water (the bathtub, a bowl, a shallow kiddie pool) and go fish!

EXTRA FUN

◆ Make lots of fish in different shapes and sizes.
◆ Make some more poles and have a fishing tournament with your friends.

Butter-Flyers

Flutter by, butterfly, on this nifty butter-flyer.

MATERIALS

Tyvek envelope ▪ ruler ▪ pencil ▪ scissors ▪ permanent markers ▪ chenille stem ▪ clothespin (hinge type) ▪ drinking straw ▪ transparent tape ▪ string (kite string or cooking twine works well) ▪ pony bead

Trim a Tyvek envelope into a 5 x 10 inch rectangle. Fold it in half crosswise so you have a 5 x 5 inch square. Draw the shape of a single butterfly wing so the middle of the wing is at the fold. Then cut out the wing, unfold, and decorate with markers.

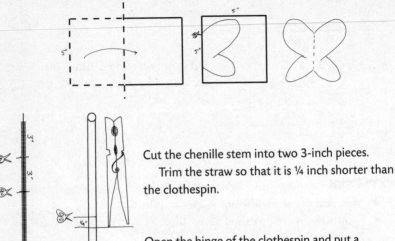

Cut the chenille stem into two 3-inch pieces. Trim the straw so that it is ¼ inch shorter than the clothespin.

Open the hinge of the clothespin and put a 3-inch piece of transparent tape inside, crosswise, centered, and sticky side facing up then let the hinge close. To make the antenna, fold one of the 3-inch pieces of chenille stem into a V shape. Lay the point of the V on the top of the clothespin so that the long ends extend beyond the clothespin jaws. Then lay the piece of straw on top of the V-shaped antenna and wrap the tape around the straw to secure the antenna and straw to the clothespin. Use another piece of tape to secure the other end of the straw to the back end of the clothespin.

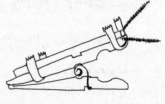

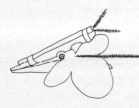

Open the clothespin again and slip the center of the butterfly wings inside, crinkling it a bit so the entire thing is between the jaws. Spiral the other 3-inch piece of chenille so it looks like a butterfly proboscis and slip that between the jaws, too.

Tie a long piece of string to a place that's a little higher than your head (for example, a banister rail of a staircase).

Slip the other end of the string, from back to front, through the straw on the butter-flyer's back. Tie a pony bead to the end so that your butter-flyer can't slip off.

Push the butter-flyer to the top of the string then walk back until the string is taut. Move the string up and down to make your butter-flyer fly toward you.

FUN FACT

Zhuangzi, an ancient Chinese philosopher, once had a dream that he was a carefree butterfly. When he woke up he didn't know if he was a man dreaming he was a butterfly or a butterfly dreaming he was a man.

Embroidery Hoop Tambourine

Personalize this tambourine with your own drawing, then jingle-jangle the day away.

MATERIALS

5-inch embroidery hoop (balsa wood or colorful plastic) ■ Tyvek envelope ■ permanent markers ■ scissors ■ four medium-sized binder clips (black or funky metallic colors) ■ eight jingle bells

Unscrew the top nut on the embroidery hoop to separate the two hoops.

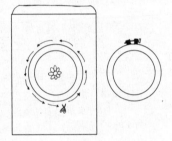

Cut open the Tyvek envelope and trim out a large piece with no seam. Trace the hoop without the top nut onto the Tyvek. Then draw another circle around this one that is wider than the first by 2 inches all around. (Don't sweat this; it doesn't have to be perfect. If you're doing it freehand, you can use a ruler to measure out 2 inches from the first circle, in eight different directions, making a dot each time. Connect these dots to draw the outside circle.) Cut around the outside circle. This will be the drumhead for the tambourine. Decorate the Tyvek drumhead with markers.

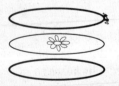

Center the drumhead (with the drawing facing up) over the embroidery hoop without the nut, then press the top hoop down over it. Tighten the screw a bit. Tug the ends of the Tyvek down so the drumhead is taut and snug, then tighten the screw as much as you can.

Remove the arms from a binder clip by pinching the sides of the arms toward one another. Slip a jingle bell over one arm, then pinch together again to reattach to the clip; slip a bell over the other arm the same way. Repeat for the other binder clips.

Attach the binder clips around the hoop and shake your groove thang!

EXTRA FUN

- ◆ Try different-sized embroidery hoops.
- ◆ Attach other kinds of bells or jingly objects (keys, paper clips, bigger or smaller bells, etc.).
- ◆ Make all the musical instruments in this book with your friends and form your own band.

FUN FACT

Most ancient cultures had their own forms of tambourines, and they were usually played by women during celebrations.

Double-Sided Drum

If you don't want to work, bang on this drum all day.

MATERIALS

wide, flat ribbon (1- to 3-inch-wide grosgrain works nicely) ▪ ruler ▪ scissors ▪ cardboard oatmeal container ▪ markers ▪ utility knife ▪ duct tape ▪ ¼ cup rice or dried beans ▪ Tyvek envelope ▪ construction paper ▪ transparent tape

Measure and cut the ribbon so that it goes around your neck and both ends reach to the bottom of your ribs, plus 2 inches.

On the side of your container make a mark 2 inches from the bottom. Then make another mark in line with the first one, 2 inches from the top of the container.

Use a utility knife to cut a slit, perpendicular to the top and bottom, at each of these marks. The slit should be the same length as the width of your ribbon.

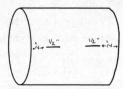

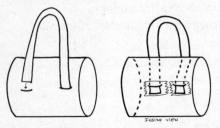

Press the cardboard gently in order to slip one end of the ribbon through one of the slits. Pull 1 inch of the ribbon through to the inside of the carton. Do the same for the other slit, making sure you don't twist the ribbon.

Lay the ribbon ends flat against the inside of the carton and cover with a 3-inch piece of duct tape, being sure to cover both the ribbon and the slit in the cardboard.

Pour ¼ cup of rice or dried beans inside the carton.

To make the drumhead, cut out a large section of the Tyvek envelope. Place the cardboard container on top of the Tyvek and use a marker to draw a circle around the perimeter.

Draw another circle 2 inches around the outside of the first. (Don't sweat this one. It doesn't have to be perfect. If you're doing it freehand, you can use a ruler to measure out 2 inches from the first circle, in eight different directions, making a dot each time. Connect these dots to draw the outside circle.)

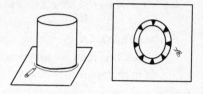

Every 2 inches around the perimeter of the Tyvek circle, cut a small triangular notch that extends to the original circle you drew.

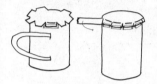

Put the head on top of the open side of the carton, lining up the original circle with the rim. Pull down each tab and secure with a small piece of duct tape all the way around the container. (Hint: Tape down a tab, then do the one opposite, so you can pull the head taut. Continue in this way until all tabs are taped down.)

To reinforce the head, run a long piece of duct tape around all the tabs on the entire perimeter of the container.

If you want your drum to look pretty, cut a piece of construction paper that will fit around the container. Tape one edge down by the ribbon, roll the paper around the carton to the other side of the ribbon, and secure with more transparent tape. Decorate with markers.

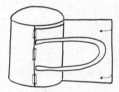

To play, put the strap over your head so the drum hangs in front of your chest. Use a couple of sticks (such as chopsticks or unsharpened pencils) or rubber band and pencil mallets (page 144) to play both sides of the drum (the Tyvek head and the cardboard bottom). Shimmy and shake to rattle the rice inside.

EXTRA FUN

◆ Make all the musical instruments in this book with your friends and form your own band.

Baby Doll

This is a great no-sew project for doll lovers.

MATERIALS
Tyvek envelope ▪ permanent markers ▪ scissors ▪ stapler
(a mini stapler with colored staples works nicely) ▪ polyfill

Cut open the envelope then fold it in half with the printing
on the inside. On the plain white side, draw the outline of
the baby doll (or use the template on page 216).

Cut out the baby doll,
going through both layers at once.
    Use permanent markers to decorate the
front and back of the baby doll.

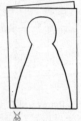

Place the front and back together. Starting just below the
head, staple around the edges of the doll until you get to
the other side below the head.

Stuff the doll with polyfill, using the capped end
of the markers (or an unsharpened pencil if your
markers are too fat) to work the stuffing into the
body. When the stuffing reaches the neck, stop.

Staple around both sides of the head, leaving a small space (about 1 inch) open on the top of the head.

Stuff the head with more polyfill, working it down with the marker or pencil.

Once the head is full, staple the top of the head closed.

EXTRA FUN

- ◆ Make a self-portrait doll.
- ◆ Try other shapes (such as a football, an animal, or the letters of your name).

Bendy Kitty

If you made the baby doll, step it up with this kitty, which has bendable arms and legs.

MATERIALS

Tyvek envelope ▪ pencil ▪ scissors ▪ permanent markers ▪ chenille stems ▪ transparent tape ▪ stapler (a mini stapler with colorful staples works nicely) ▪ polyfill

Fold the envelope in half with the printed side on the inside. On the plain white side, follow these steps to draw the outline of your kitty cat on one side of the envelope (or use the template on page 217 if freehand drawing's not for you):

With a pencil, lightly sketch a stick figure with a round head, long arms that stick out straight, and long legs that form a V at the bottom of the body.

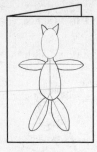

Make a big long oval for the body. Round out the arms and legs so they're at least ½ inch thick. Add triangle-shaped ears to the top of the head.

Cut out two kitties (by cutting through both the front and the back of the envelope at the same time).

Use permanent markers to decorate the front and back of the cat. (Draw a face and paws, and color in the arms, legs, and belly. Give it spots or stripes and a tail.) Then set the front aside.

Form one chenille stem into an upside-down V and use transparent tape to secure it to the legs on the inside surface of the back piece of the cat.

Tape a straight stem across both arms.

Tape a third straight stem on the body between the arms and legs.

Use another stem for the neck and head.

Finally, use two tiny pieces of stems for the ears.

Lay the front of the cat (decorated side up) over the back, making sure the chenille stems are in between the layers. Starting just below the neck on one side, staple around the outside edges of the arm, down the side of the body, around each leg, up the other side of the body, and around the other arm. Now, only the neck and head are not stapled.

Take a bit of polyfill and stuff it into the body, pushing it down gently with a pencil. Don't worry about filling the arms and legs. The chenille stems will give them form.

Once the body is stuffed, staple around the sides of the face, then stop and push polyfill into the head.

Continue stapling around the ears and the top of the head.
    Bend your kitty into different positions.

EXTRA FUN

◆ Make different critters (dogs, frogs, pigs, goats, people, etc.) or a robot.
◆ Make your critters a cozy place to live out of a cardboard box (see the box barn with cork horses as an example on page 31).

Sled Kite and String Spool

Because Tyvek is hard to tear and water resistant, it's a great material for a sturdy homemade kite like this one.

MATERIALS
Tyvek envelope (11 x 15 inches) ▪ scissors ▪ permanent markers ▪ ruler ▪ hole punch ▪ paper reinforcement circles ▪ four bamboo skewers ▪ transparent tape ▪ string ▪ empty spool ▪ two rubber bands ▪ unsharpened pencil or round chopstick

To Make the Kite

Cut the flap off the Tyvek mailer, then cut down the center seam on the back and across the bottom seam, leaving the side seams intact so the envelope splays open. Label the seams A and B.

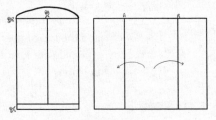

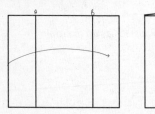

Fold the opened envelope in half, lining up seams A and B, so that the printed side is facing in, A is on top, and the fold is on the left side of the envelope.

On the right side (where the edges come together), measure and mark 5 inches from the top. Draw a straight line diagonally from this dot to the top of seam A. Then draw a straight line from this dot diagonally to the bottom of seam A. Cut along these lines.

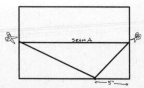

On the left side (where the fold is) draw half of a 3-inch-tall heart; start it 9 inches from the top and finish it 3 inches from the bottom. Cut out the heart.

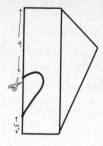

Open the envelope.

Punch holes in the corners of flap A and flap B. Reinforce these holes with paper circles. (If you don't have these, cover the corners with a piece of transparent tape, then punch holes through the tape and envelope.) Decorate the kite with permanent markers if you want.

Trim the pointy ends off the bamboo skewers, then measure and cut them to run the length of seam A and seam B. Secure the skewers with long pieces of transparent tape.

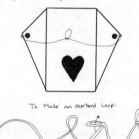

To make the bridle, cut a 2-yard length of string. Tie one end through the hole on flap A and the other end through the hole in flap B. Tie an overhand loop in the center of the string.

To Make an overhand Loop:

To Make a String Spool

Tie the end of your ball of string around the empty spool and secure with tape.

Wind lots of string around the spool, then cut. Tie the free end to the loop on the bridle.

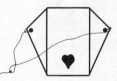

Wind one rubber band over one end of the pencil. Slide the spool over the other end of the pencil. Wind the other rubber band around the other end of the pencil. Push the rubber bands near the spool to keep it from slipping off the pencil.

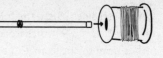

Go fly a kite!

EXTRA FUN

- ◆ Use different-sized envelopes to make smaller or bigger kites.
- ◆ Cut out different shapes in the center (such as a circle, triangle, star, or fish).
- ◆ Decorate your kites in fantastic ways.
- ◆ Add a tail made from long strips of plastic sacks.

FUN FACT

In 1822, George Pocock invented a carriage that could be pulled by two kites instead of horses.

WIRE HANGER PROJECTS

THE HUMBLE WIRE hanger often gets overlooked as dry cleaner detritus, but most of us have a few of them hanging around our houses anyway. They're great for toy making because the wire is easy to manipulate and the waxed cardboard tube across the bottom is durable.

FACTS ABOUT HANGERS

- For most of history people hung their clothes on hooks or laid them flat in drawers or cupboards for storage.
- Some people think Thomas Jefferson invented the wooden hanger, but no one knows for sure.
- Albert J. Parkhouse received the first patent for a wire hanger, in 1903. He made the hanger because his coworkers at Timberlake Wire and Novelty Company complained that there weren't enough hooks to hang their coats.
- In 1932, Schuyler C. Hulett patented a hanger with cardboard tubes to help prevent wrinkles.

Magic Wand

You can make magic wands out of so many things but the fairies I know like this version because it's simple, sturdy, and jingly.

MATERIALS

curling ribbon used for wrapping presents (several colors)
■ ruler ■ scissors ■ long chenille stem ■ dry cleaner hanger
with a cardboard tube ■ jingle bell

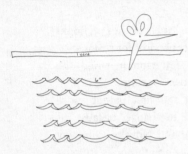

Cut six 1-yard lengths of ribbon in various colors. Use one leg of the scissors to curl the ends, leaving the center 6 inches straight.

Put all the ribbons together and lay on a flat work surface. Put the chenille stem perpendicular to the center of the ribbons. Loop the top 2 inches of the stem around the ribbons and twist the stem around on itself tightly.

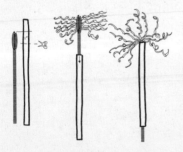

You need only the cardboard tube off the bottom of the hanger for this project, so remove the wire part of the hanger and set it aside for something else. Trim the cardboard tube so it is 1

inch shorter than the new length of the chenille stem. Slip the chenille stem through the tube and pull it down so only the ribbons stick out of the top.

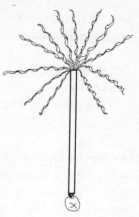

Last, twist the jingle bell around the end of the stem that's sticking out of the bottom of the cardboard tube.

Cast a spell!

EXTRA FUN

◆ If you want to make your wand fancier, decorate the cardboard tube with stickers, markers, glitter glue, etc. (Note: Some hanger tubes are coated with wax, which means the decorations won't stick very well. If that's the case, you can lightly sand the tube before decorating.)

◆ Make a set of fancy fairy wings (page 194) or no-sew butterfly wings (page 128) to go with your wand.

FUN FACT

The Great Book of Saint Cyprian, *published in 1849, has step-by-step instructions for how to make a magic wand.*

Whimmy Doodle

Whimmy Doodles are old Appalachian toys and make excellent propellers for imaginary airplanes.

MATERIALS

wire hanger ■ wire cutters or strong scissors ■ jingle bell ■ needle-nose pliers ■ corrugated cardboard scraps ■ ruler ■ wooden pencil

Use the wire cutters or strong scissors to snip the wire hanger so that you end up with the hook of the hanger plus one long side.

Bend the hook down so you have one long straight piece with a handle at one end. Attach a jingle bell to the opposite end and use the needle-nose pliers to loop the wire closed so the bell stays in place. (If you have a small piece of hanger poking out from under the handle, use the pliers to twist it closed, too.)

Cut out a 1½ x 4 inch rectangle of corrugated cardboard and punch a hole in the center to make the propeller. Slip the propeller over the handle and down the wire to the bell.

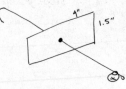

4"

1.5"

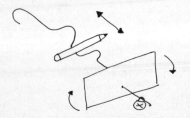

Bend the wire to create two large bumps in the middle. Hold the handle of the hanger with one hand while with the other you quickly run the pencil at a slight angle back and forth along the bumps. Watch your whimmy doodle twirl!

EXTRA FUN

◆ Cut different lengths and shapes for propellers (for example, a long, thin oval or a diamond).

◆ Decorate the propeller with markers. Notice how designs change as the propeller spins.

◆ Try more than one propeller at one time.

◆ Tilt the pencil slightly to the right or left as you rub it against the wire to see if you can make the propeller change directions.

FUN FACT

Whimmy doodles have lots of names, such as propeller sticks, hooey sticks, gee-haws, Ouija windmills, voodoo sticks, and whammy diddles. They were originally made of wood.

Mama and Baby Bird Whirligig

Whirligigs are usually made with a windmill attachment so they spin outside, but in this version, a hand crank turns the mama and baby birds pecking at seeds.

MATERIALS

flimsy wire hanger ▪ needle-nose pliers ▪ four rubber bands ▪ adult-sized shoe box with lid* ▪ ruler ▪ pencil ▪ utility knife ▪ pushpin ▪ scissors ▪ markers and/or construction paper, feathers, glue (optional) ▪ hole punch ▪ two prong paper fasteners ▪ two chenille stems ▪ masking tape

* Note: I made this project from a 7 x 11 inch shoe box, but you could use any size; just adjust the measurements to fit your box. Also, if you don't have needle-nose pliers that also cut wire, you can use strong, heavy-duty scissors to cut and shape the hanger.

To Make the Box and Crank Arm

Use the wire cutters on the pliers to remove the hook from the hanger, then straighten the hanger out as much as possible.

Wrap a rubber band around each end of the hanger and push them toward the center for now.

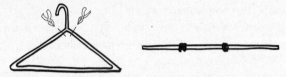

Now use the needle-nose part of the pliers to help shape the hanger into the following configuration, with the rubber bands pushed back again toward each end when you're done.

Remove the lid from the shoe box and set it aside for later. Turn the box upside down so that the bottom of the box becomes the top of the whirligig. Measure, mark, and cut out (using your utility knife) two 2 x 3 inch rectangles centered on the box and 2 inches apart. The long sides of the cutout rectangles should be parallel to the short sides of the box.

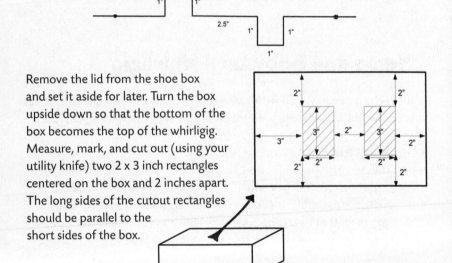

On a short side of the box, measure and mark the midpoint (3½ inches from each side, if it's a 7-inch-wide box), 1 inch from the top of the whirligig. Poke the pushpin through this dot to make a small hole. Do the same on the other short side.

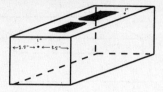

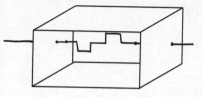

From the inside of the box, push one end of the hanger through the hole in one side of the box. Push it through far enough that you can put the other end of the hanger through the hole on the other side. (Note: The rubber bands should be on the inside of the box.)

Set the box on your workspace so the cutaway rectangles are on top again. Center the hanger so that the 90-degree bends are squarely visible inside each cutaway rectangle.

Push the rubber bands so that each is snug against its corresponding inside wall of the box.

Wind the remaining two rubber bands around the ends of the hangers sticking out of the box. Push these rubber bands to make them snug against the outside walls of the box.

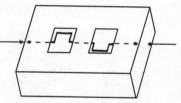

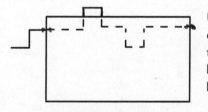

Use the wire cutters to trim one end of the hanger down to ½ inch, then use the needle-nose part to bend the hanger over so it's no longer pointy.

On the left side, create a crank.

To Make the Birds

Cut the rim off the top of the box and discard it.

Draw one 7-inch bird and one 5-inch bird, and their legs, on the box top

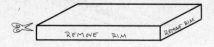

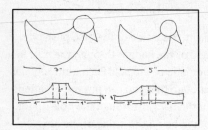

(or use the templates on pages 218–220). Cut these pieces out. Score the legs along the dotted lines (this will make the birds stand upright).

Decorate the birds with markers or construction paper or even feathers if you want.

Punch a hole under the wing of each bird and one on the chest.

Fold the legs and punch a hole in the top of each leg as shown.

For each bird attach the legs to the hole under the wing with a prong paper fastener.

Run a chenille stem through the hole on the chest. Fold the stem in half and twist it tightly, leaving ½ inch of stem on each side.

With a long side of the whirligig facing you, position the birds on the box so that the mama bird's toes line up just to the left of the cutaway rectangle on your left and the baby bird's toes line up just to the right of the cutaway rectangle on your right. Secure the birds' feet with a bit of masking tape.

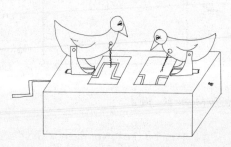

Turn the crank until the bent hanger stands upright in the cutout rectangle below the mama bird. Stand the mama bird up straight and twist the end of the chenille stem around the center of the bent hanger. (To keep the stem from sliding back and forth along the hanger, wind a bit of masking tape around the hanger on each side of the bend.)

Stand the baby bird upright and crank the handle once so the bent hanger on that side comes up. Twist the baby bird's chenille stem around the center of this part of the hanger. (As with the other side, to keep the stem from sliding back and forth along the hanger, wind a bit of tape around each side of the bend in the hanger.)

Decorate the box if you want, then turn the crank and watch the birds peck at the ground.

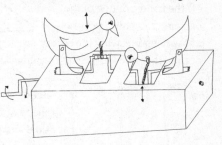

EXTRA FUN

- ◆ Glue birdseed to the center of the whirligig where the birds peck.
- ◆ Make a worm peeking out of the center of the box where the birds peck.
- ◆ Try making different scenes, such as two people hammering on a nail or two kids jumping on a trampoline.

FUN FACT

The word "whirligig" comes from the old English words "whirlen" (to whirl) and "gigg" (top), so it literally means to whirl a top.

Fancy Fairy Wings

These wings are more complicated than the no-sew butterfly version on page 128, but they're lovely and will last a long time. However, you don't have to know how to sew to make them. I've included a no-sew option for putting the wings together.

> **⫼⫼⫼ MATERIALS** ⫼⫼⫼
> two wire hangers ▪ wire cutters ▪ duct tape ▪ panty hose (bigger is better) ▪ scissors ▪ 12 x 12 inch square of felt ▪ ruler ▪ pencil or chalk ▪ ½-inch-wide flat elastic braid ▪ needle and thread (or four safety pins) ▪ fabric glue ▪ glitter ▪ sequins and sparkly beads (optional)

Use the wire cutters to cut off the handle of one of the hangers. Straighten out one side of the hanger, leaving the corner

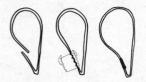

of the other side intact. This corner will be the bottom point of the wing.

Bend the other end of the hanger into the shape of the top of the wing. This takes some time and patience. Keep working the hanger until you've got the desired shape.

Next, attach the ends of the hanger by using the tip of the wire cutters to twist one end around the other, then secure with duct tape.

Repeat this process for the other hanger, getting the two wings as close to the same shape as possible.

Cut the legs off the panty hose. The next step is to stretch one leg over each wire wing. This will take some coaxing. The bigger the panty hose, the better. But you may also need to spend some time stretching the hose with your hands before you can work it over the wire frame. As long as you work carefully and slowly, you

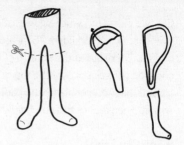

shouldn't get any runs in the hose. (If you do get a run, paint over it with clear fingernail polish and let it dry or stitch it up with needle and thread.) You may also need to re-form the frame once you get the hose over.

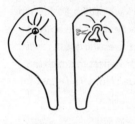

Once the panty hose have loosened up and are in place and the frame keeps it shape, tie the open end of the hose into a small, tight knot on the back of the wing. Trim off any excess fabric. Repeat for the other wing.

Cut two 6 x 6 inch felt squares. Fold one square in half, side to side. On the folded edge, measure down 1 inch from the top. Use a ruler to draw a straight line from the top outer corner to that mark, then cut along the line. Repeat on the bottom. When you unfold the felt it should look like the illustration below. Cut the other piece of felt to match exactly. These pieces will hold the wings together so they can flap. Set these aside.

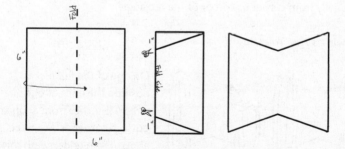

Cut two pieces of ½-inch-wide elastic that will fit over your fairy's shoulders. To measure around one shoulder, start at the bottom of the armpit and loop your elastic over the top of the shoulder, around the shoulder blade, and back under the armpit. Then reduce this number by 3 inches.

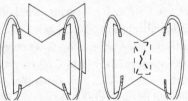

If You Can Sew

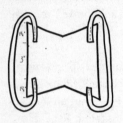

Attach both elastic straps to one of the felt flappers. To do this, position one end of an elastic 1½ inches from a top corner. Attach with a quick whipstitch. Position the other end of the elastic 1½ inches from the bottom corner below it, making sure the elastic doesn't twist. Attach with a quick whipstitch. Repeat to attach the second elastic to the other side. (Note: The ends of the elastic should be about 3 inches apart.)

Now lay the felt with the elastic attached on top of the other piece of felt and pin together. (The elastic should be on top, facing up.) Stitch a 2 x 3 inch rectangle in the center of the felt, then stitch diagonally from corner to corner of the rectangle.

If Sewing's Not Your Bag

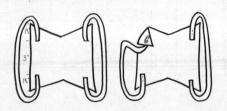

On one of the felt pieces, position the ends of one elastic strap 1½ inches from a top and bottom corner as described above. From underneath this piece, attach with safety pins,

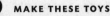

so that the elastic is on top of the felt and the safety pins are hidden underneath. The ends of the elastic should be about 3 inches apart. Repeat to attach the second elastic to the other side.

On the other piece of felt, put fabric glue over the center 2 inches from top to bottom. Lay the piece with the elastic attached on top of that (with the safety pins between the layers and the elastic on top). Put a heavy book on top and let dry completely.

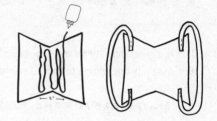

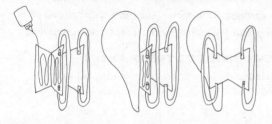

To attach the wings to the felt flappers, for both the sewn and nonsewn variety:

Fold one top flap back. Cover the facing surfaces of the two layers with fabric glue. Center the interior edge of a wing between the flaps and close the top flap, sandwiching the wing between the felt layers. Top with a book to dry. Do the same for the other side.

To decorate your wings, make pretty designs with fabric glue and top with glitter. Or, if you're feeling really crafty, make flowers and leaves out of scraps of felt and sew them on the wings. Add sequins or sparkly beads. When your fairy is ready to don her wings, slip the elastic straps over her shoulders and watch her flit about.

EXTRA FUN

◆ If your fairy is magic, make the magic wand on page 186.

Five Mix-'n'-Match Shakers

This is a great activity for a group. Lay all the materials on a work surface and let everyone mix and match materials to create different kinds of shakers.

MATERIALS FOR THE OUTSIDE OF THE SHAKERS

plastic egg ▪ cardboard tube (toilet paper, paper towel, or wrapping paper tube) ▪ tin can (unopened and containing something liquid, like tomato sauce) ▪ cardboard container (such as a bread crumb or oatmeal container) ▪ plastic jug with a handle (empty, clean, and dry)

MATERIALS FOR THE INSIDE OF THE SHAKERS

dried chickpeas ▪ dried lentils ▪ dried navy beans ▪ jingle bells ▪ rice

EXTRA STUFF

can opener ▪ construction paper ▪ duct tape ▪ markers and stickers ▪ masking tape ▪ scissors ▪ stapler ▪ transparent tape

Plastic Egg Shaker

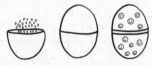

1. Fill half of one shell.
2. Put the other half on top.
3. Reinforce the seam with masking tape.
4. Decorate with stickers or permanent markers.

Cardboard Tube Shaker

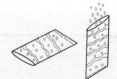

1. Flatten the tube and decorate with markers, stickers, etc.
2. Staple one end closed.

3. Fill halfway.

4. Staple the other end closed.

Tin Can Shaker

1. Remove the label then make a hole in the lid with a can opener. Pour the contents into a storage container and refrigerate for later, then rinse the can and let it dry completely.

2. Put a few tablespoons of filling inside. (If you have trouble getting the filling in, make a small funnel by rolling up a piece of paper and sticking an end in the opening.)

3. Cover the hole with duct tape.

4. Cut a piece of construction paper so that it will fit around the outside of the can.

5. Decorate the paper.

6. Use transparent tape to secure one end of the construction paper to the can. Wrap the paper around the can and tape the other end.

Cardboard Container Shaker

1. Remove the lid and, if possible, the label.

2. Put in a few tablespoons to a half cup of filling, depending on the size of the container.

3. Replace the lid and secure with masking tape around the edge.

4. Cut a piece of construction paper so that it will fit around the outside of the container.
5. Decorate the paper.
6. Use transparent tape to secure one end of the paper to the container. Wrap the paper around the container and tape the other end.

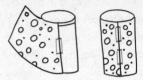

Plastic Jug Shaker

1. Remove the cap and, if possible, the label, then rinse the jug and cap and let them dry completely.
2. Put in a few tablespoons to a half cup of filling, depending on the size of the jug.
3. Decorate the jug and lid with stickers and permanent markers.
4. Replace the lid.

EXTRA FUN

◆ Make all the musical instruments in this book with your friends and form your own band.

Recipes for Crafty Old Standbys

ANY TOY BOOK worth its salt dough should have some tried-and-true recipes for fun. The kitchen cupboard is a great place to explore for inspiration. Most of these recipes have been circulating for years. Others are newer. But all of them are low cost and big fun.

Quick No-Cook Salt Dough

This is the quickest and easiest of the play doughs; kids can even whip it up on their own. This dough doesn't last long and will harden if left out, so store it in an airtight container (you can also put it in the fridge) for up to a few days.

> **MATERIALS**
> 1 cup flour ▪ ¼ cup salt ▪ ¼ to ½ cup water ▪ mixing bowl
> ▪ spoon

1. Mix the flour and salt in a bowl.
2. Add ¼ cup of the water and stir until water is absorbed.
3. Drizzle in more water, stirring and kneading the dough with your hands, until the dough is the consistency you want.

EXTRA FUN
◆ Roll it out and cut it into shapes, then let them air-dry or pop them in a low-temperature oven (200 degrees Fahrenheit) on an ungreased cookie sheet for half an hour. Once they are dry, paint with tempera paint.

◆ Make them into hanging decorations by poking a hole in the top of each shape and looping a ribbon through.

No-Cook Oatmeal Dough

This is another quick and easy modeling dough that kids can make themselves. It's softer than the salt dough (it smells nice, too) so it's easier for small hands to manipulate. It will keep for a day or two in an airtight container.

MATERIALS
1 cup flour ▪ 2 cups rolled oats ▪ 1 cup water ▪ mixing bowl ▪ spoon

1. Mix oatmeal and flour in the bowl.
2. Slowly add water as you stir.
3. Knead until the dough is the consistency you want.

Cooked Play Dough

Many a rainy afternoon has been saved by play dough. This cooked version will last for months in an airtight container, but you'll need to make it at least a few hours before you want to play with it since it has to cool.

MATERIALS
3 cups flour ▪ 1½ cups salt ▪ 6 teaspoons cream of tartar ▪ 3 tablespoons vegetable oil ▪ 3 cups water ▪ few drops of food coloring ▪ cooking pot ▪ spoon ▪ bowl

1. Mix all ingredients together in a cooking pot over medium-low heat.
2. Stir continually until the dough pulls away from the sides of the pot.
3. Continue stirring for another minute until the dough begins to form a ball.
4. Put dough into a bowl to cool.

5. Once it's cool, knead the dough for a few minutes to get the desired consistency.
6. Store in an airtight container.

EXTRA FUN
- ◆ Make two half batches, each a different color.

Sugar Bubbles

The corn syrup in these bubbles makes them shiny and beautiful. They're almost like mirrored orbs floating in your garden.

MATERIALS

3 cups water ▪ ½ cup light corn syrup (such as Karo) ▪ 1 cup dishwashing liquid ▪ jar with a lid

1. Combine the ingredients in the jar, close the lid tight, and swirl gently to blend (without foaming up the soap).

Glycerin Bubbles

If you come across vegetable glycerin in the grocery or pharmacy, pick up a small bottle. These bubbles are strong and last longer than the kind you buy at the store.

MATERIALS

3 cups water ▪ ½ cup dishwashing liquid ▪ 1½ tablespoons vegetable glycerin ▪ jar with a lid

1. Combine the ingredients in the jar, close the lid tight, and swirl gently to blend (without foaming up the soap).

Drinking Straw Bubble Pipe

MATERIALS

different-sized drinking straws (e.g., flexible, bubble tea, and coffee stirrers) ▪ shallow plastic bowl or lid (such as from a butter tub) ▪ bubble liquid (see recipes on page 203)

1. Pour the bubble liquid into the shallow plastic bowl or lid.
2. Dip one end of a drinking straw in the liquid.
3. Blow gently on the other end to use your bubble pipe.

Paper Clip Bubble Wand

MATERIALS

different-sized paper clips ▪ needle-nose pliers ▪ bubble liquid (see recipes on page 203)

1. Use the needle-nose pliers to bend the top half of a paper clip into the shape of a circle.
2. Straighten out the bottom half for the handle.
3. Dip into the bubble liquid and blow gently.

EXTRA FUN

◆ Try making different shapes, such as a triangle, a square, or a figure 8.

Million-Bubble Blower

MATERIALS

plastic water bottle ▪ old sock ▪ rubber band ▪ scissors ▪ bubble liquid (see recipes on page 203) ▪ shallow bowl

1. Cut the bottom end off a plastic water bottle and discard, keeping the part with the drinking spout.
2. Cut the heel and ankle off an old thick sock and discard. Put the toe end of the sock over the cut end of the bottle. Pull the sock tight and secure with a rubber band.

3. Pour bubble liquid into a shallow bowl.
4. Dip the sock end of the blower in the liquid. Blow through the drinking spout to make million-bubble clusters come through the sock.

invisible inks

Spies can write secret messages with any number of handy "inks." Each of these is heat activated, meaning the person who receives the message will have to heat up the paper to reveal the message.

FOR THE INK, USE ONE OF THE FOLLOWING:
lemon juice ▪ potato juice ▪ onion juice ▪ 1 tablespoon baking soda plus 1 tablespoon water ▪ vinegar

FOR THE WRITING INSTRUMENT, USE ONE OF THE FOLLOWING:
toothpick ▪ small paintbrush ▪ cotton swab

1. Write your message on a piece of ordinary paper. Let dry so the message disappears.
2. To reveal the message, place the paper under a warm (not hot) iron or hold it up to a 100-watt bulb.

Milk Paint

Before Sherwin-Williams came along, people used real milk paint, made with lime, to give wood a beautiful finish. This simple version, using powdered milk and food coloring, is great for painting cardboard or paper. It has a soft, pretty finish and won't smell once it's dry.

MATERIALS

½ cup water ▪ food coloring ▪ ½ cup powdered milk ▪ jar with a lid

1. Put the water and a few drops of food coloring in the jar. Add the powdered milk. Put the lid on the jar and shake until the milk is dissolved and the color is even.
2. Make lots of colors.
3. Store in the fridge for up to a week.

Condensed Milk Paint

Here's an even quicker and easier version of milk paint that works well on cardboard or paper.

MATERIALS

can of condensed milk ▪ food coloring ▪ small jars with lids

1. Put ¼ cup of the condensed milk into a jar. Add a drop or two of food coloring. Put the lid on and shake. Make other colors in the other jars.
2. Store in the fridge for up to a week.

Glitter Gel Paint

These gel paints are bright and sparkly and dry easily. Use them to decorate cardboard or paper creations.

MATERIALS

4 tablespoons light corn syrup (such as Karo) ▪ 1½ teaspoons dishwashing liquid ▪ food coloring ▪ glitter ▪ small containers with lids

1. Mix the corn syrup and dish soap in a container. Add a few drops of food coloring. Pour in glitter. Mix.
2. Make lots of different colors.
3. Cover tightly to store for up to a week.

Glossary

bamboo skewer: thin, 12- to 18-inch pointed wooden stick used to make shish kebabs

binder clip: a metal clip with two arms, used for binding stacks of paper

chenille stem: (aka pipe cleaner) a long wire covered with short, soft polyester bristles

circular reinforcement labels: self-adhesive, circular stickers used to reinforce holes punched into paper, such as pages in a three-ring binder

craft stick: (aka tongue depressor or Popsicle stick) flat wooden stick with rounded ends; available in many sizes and colors

embroidery hoop: two wooden or plastic hoops that fit together to hold fabric taut; the outside hoop can be loosened or tightened by an attached metal screw

felt: a type of fabric that doesn't fray; usually comes in 12-inch squares or can be bought by the yard

flat braided elastic: this is the stretchy stuff you find inside waistbands; you can buy lengths of it in different colors and widths such as ½ inch

foam: you probably know this stuff by a brand name that rhymes with *pyrofoam*; it's made into paper plates, egg cartons, cups, packing peanuts, and take-out containers

foam board: a layer of foam that's been laminated on both sides

hook-and-loop fastener: you probably know this stuff as Velcro, which is a brand name (like calling tissues Kleenex); I use the kind with self-adhesive on the back

jingle bell: small metal bell with a tiny loop on the back

metal washer: a small, round metal disk used in faucets

polyfill: (aka stuffing or fiberfill) the fluffy stuff inside a pillow, which can be bought in bags at a craft or fabric store

pony bead: a small plastic bead with a flat top and bottom and a large hole in the center

prong paper fastener: (aka brad) a small brass fastener with a flat round top and two prongs for legs

pushpin: a tack with a ¼-inch-tall plastic head (in contrast to a thumbtack, which has a flat head)

round elastic cord: round cord made of stretchy elastic that you will find in fabric shops (think of the stretchy cord that holds a birthday hat below your chin)

scoring: using one leg of a pair of scissors, or a utility knife, to cut only halfway through cardboard so the cardboard will fold

spool: a flanged cylinder (usually of plastic or wood) that holds sewing thread

Tyvek envelope: Tyvek is a brand name for spunbond olefin readily available as envelopes, especially Express Mail envelopes from the post office

utility knife: (aka box cutter or carpet knife) a sharp, 3- to 4-inch razor blade held in a plastic casing

X-Acto knife: a brand name for a short, sharp blade attached to a penlike handle

Templates

Bunny Wagon

Dress-Up Doll Frame

Cutout Dress-Up Dolls

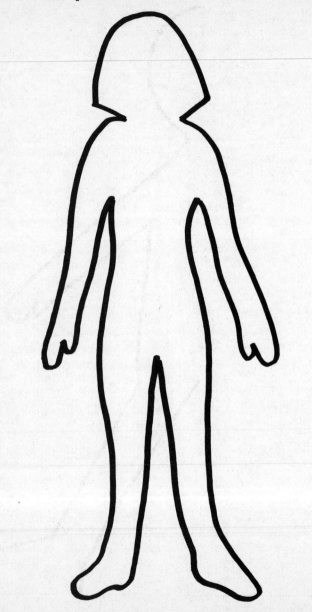

Stacking Box Face Puzzle

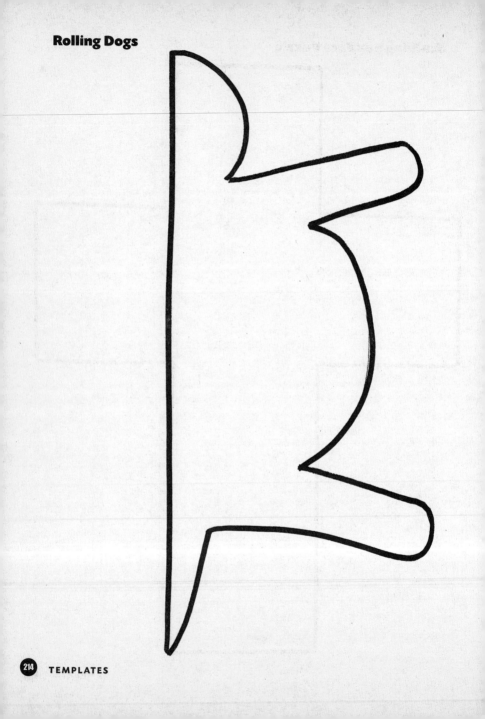

Windup Mouse

Magnetic Fish

Baby Doll

Bendy Kitty

Whirligig Mama and Baby Bird

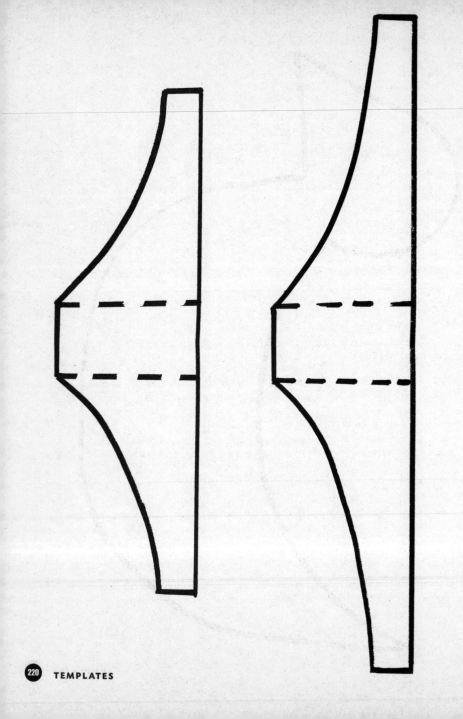

index